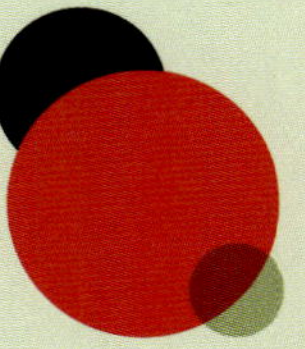

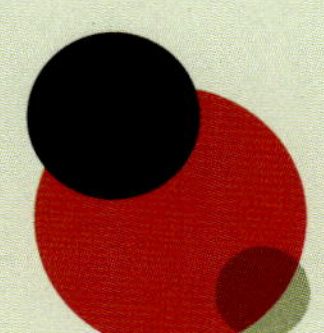

Symptomatica FALSE/POSITIVE
Published by Baby Tattoo Books® Los Angeles
www.babytattoo.com

ISBN 978-0-9793307-9-7

First edition
10 9 8 7 6 5 4 3 2 1

Manufactured in China.

Symptomatica

ragnar

- The Academy
- Bad Robot
- House Of Secrets
- Big City
- Cutthroats
- Spooketto
- Lexiconic
- Pulps

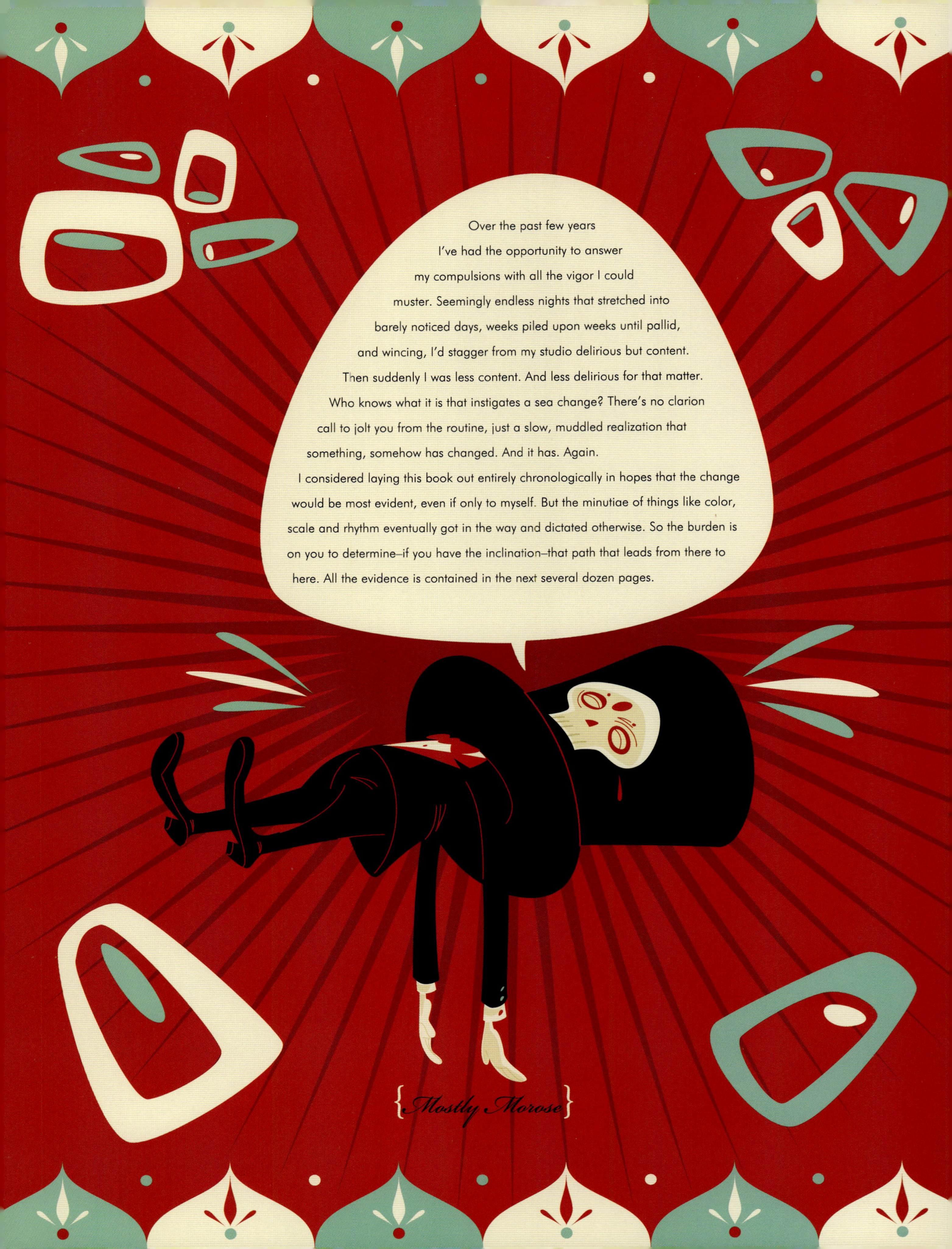

Over the past few years I've had the opportunity to answer my compulsions with all the vigor I could muster. Seemingly endless nights that stretched into barely noticed days, weeks piled upon weeks until pallid, and wincing, I'd stagger from my studio delirious but content. Then suddenly I was less content. And less delirious for that matter. Who knows what it is that instigates a sea change? There's no clarion call to jolt you from the routine, just a slow, muddled realization that something, somehow has changed. And it has. Again. I considered laying this book out entirely chronologically in hopes that the change would be most evident, even if only to myself. But the minutiae of things like color, scale and rhythm eventually got in the way and dictated otherwise. So the burden is on you to determine—if you have the inclination—that path that leads from there to here. All the evidence is contained in the next several dozen pages.
{Mostly Morose}

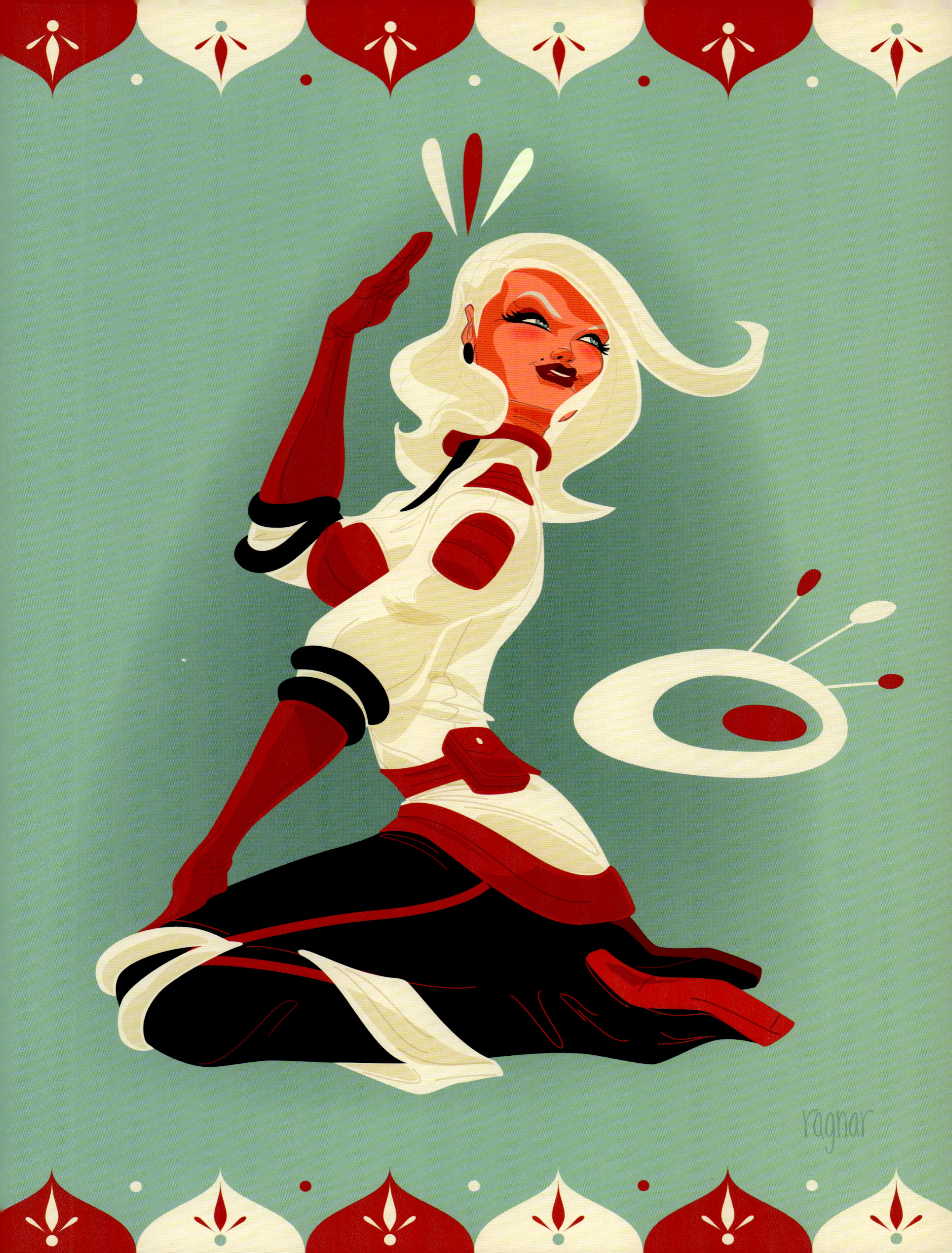
ragnar

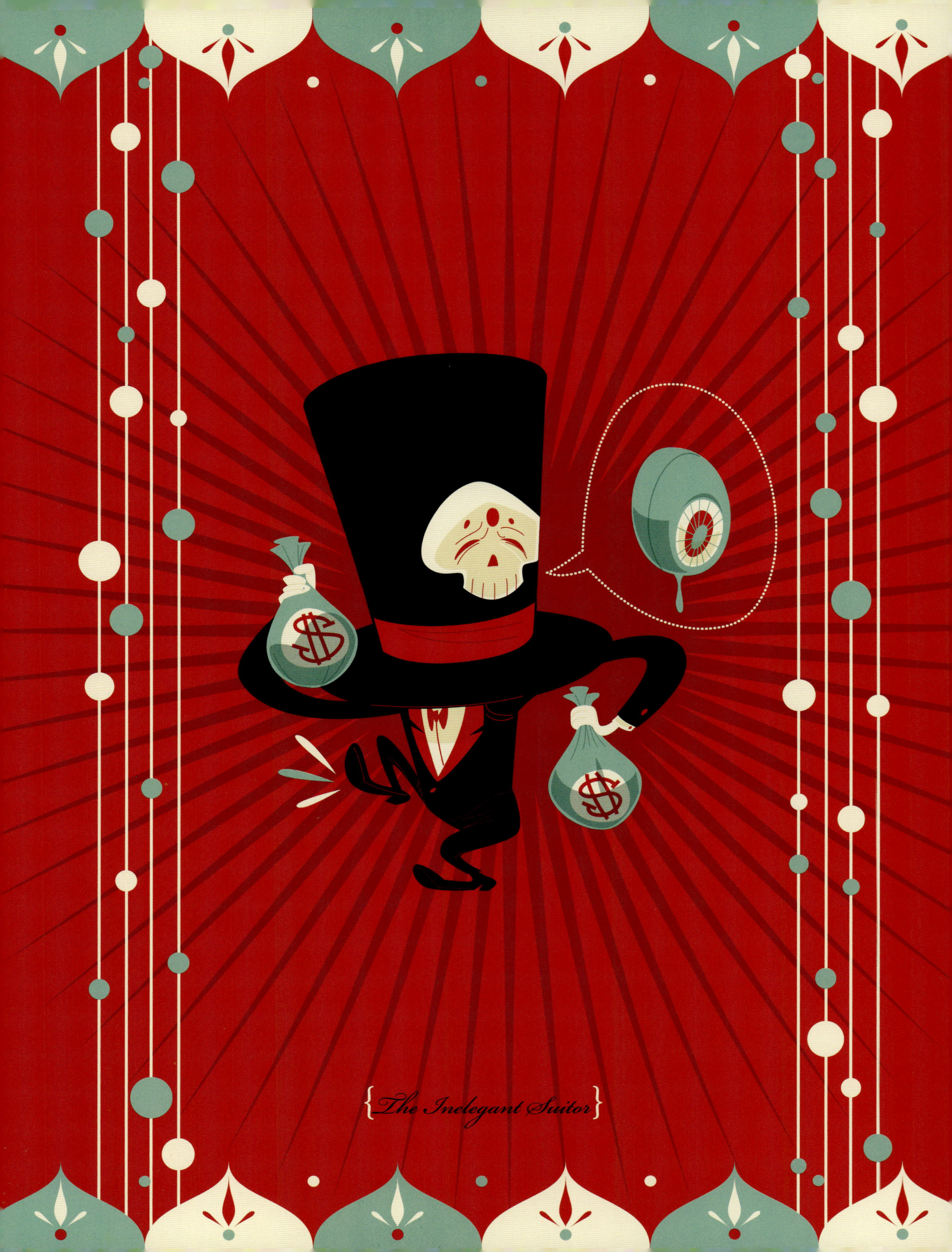

{The Inelegant Suitor}

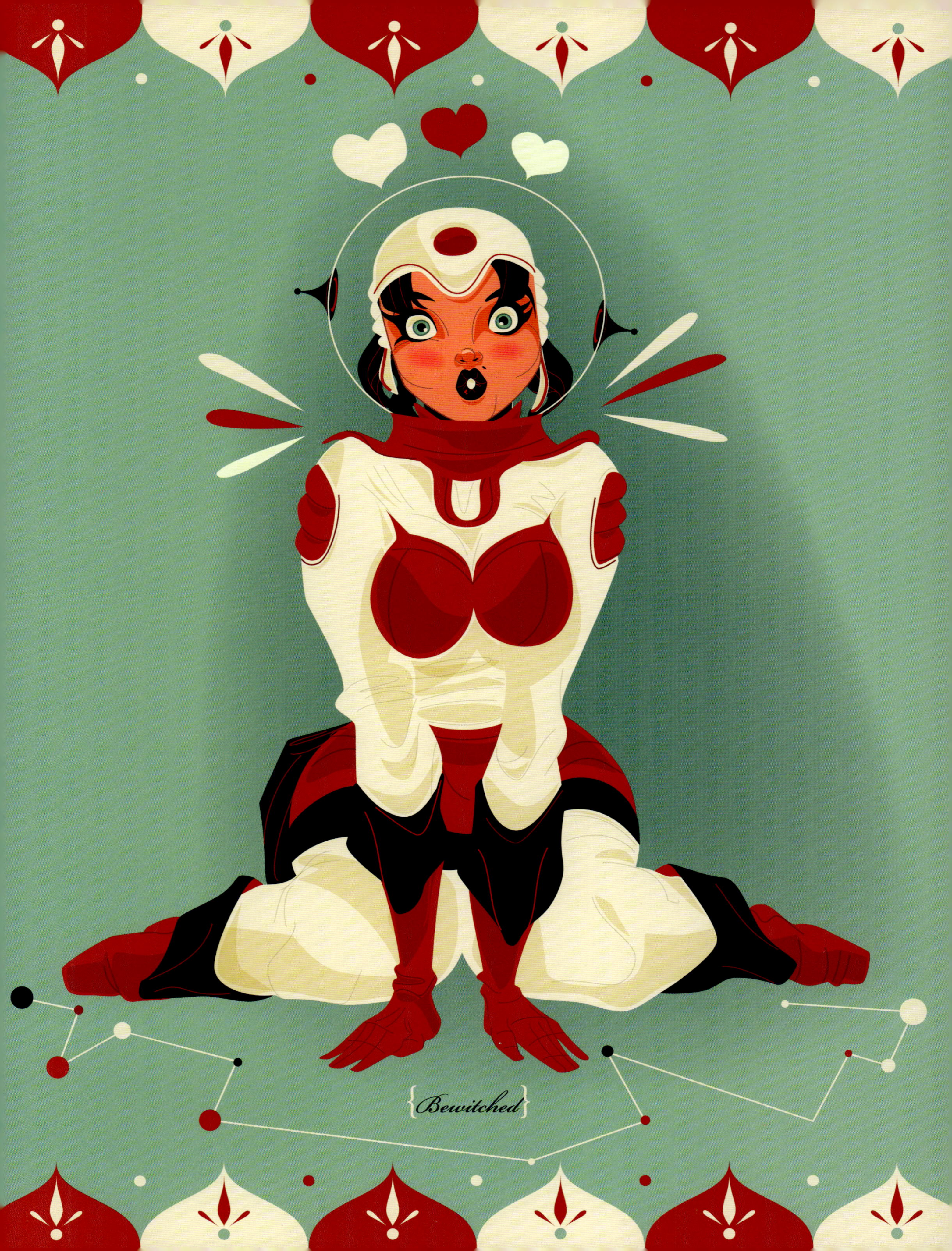

{Bewitched}

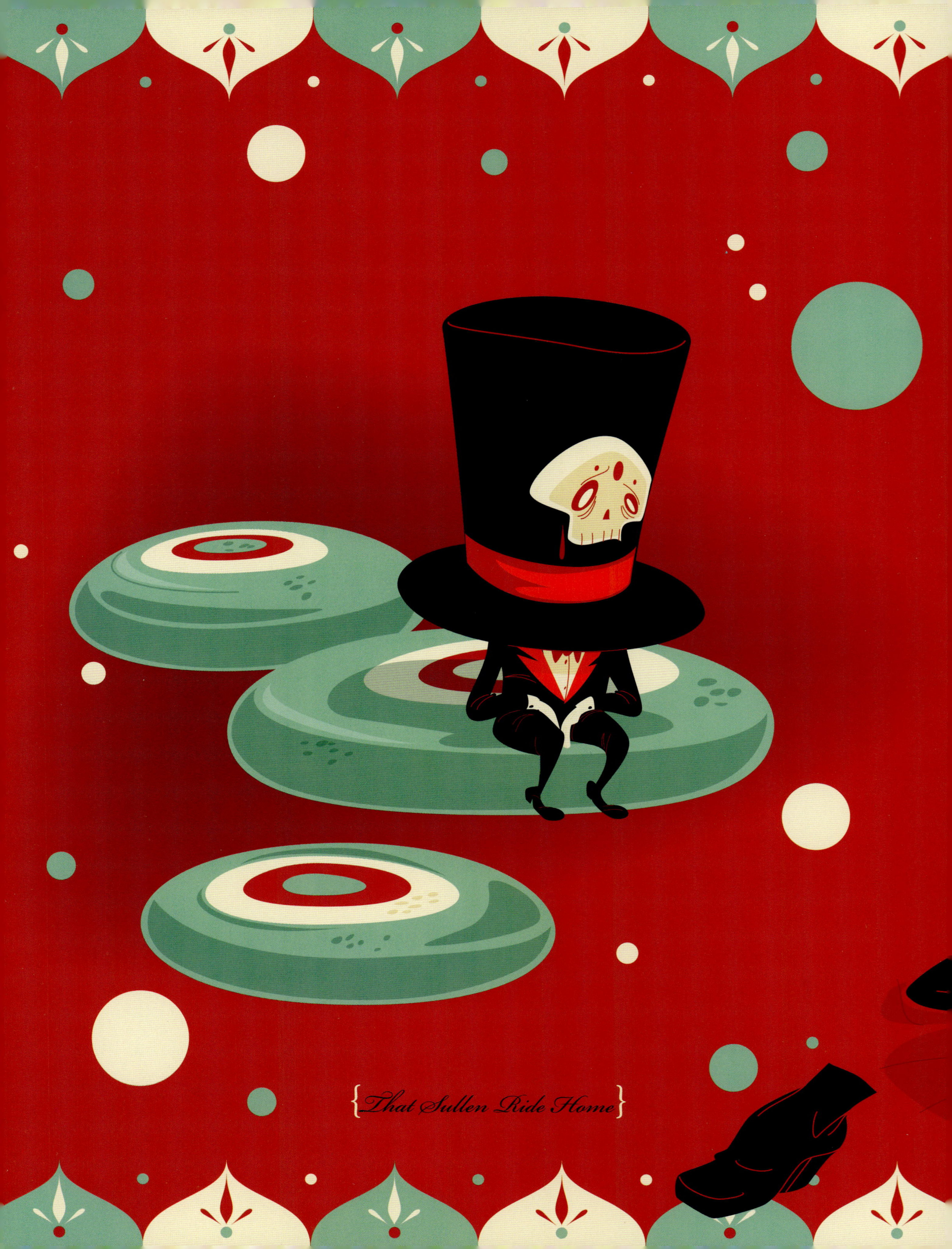
{That Sullen Ride Home}

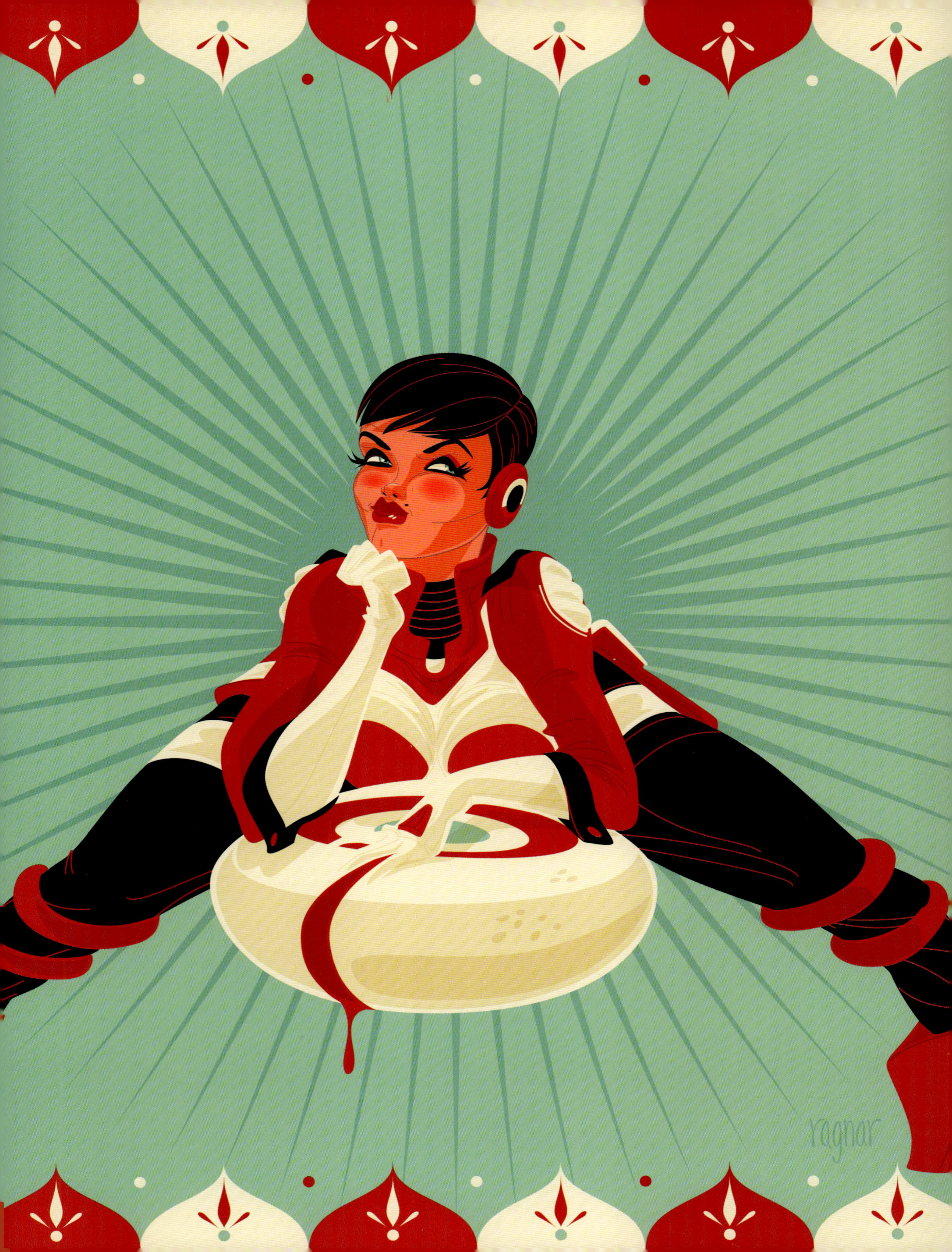

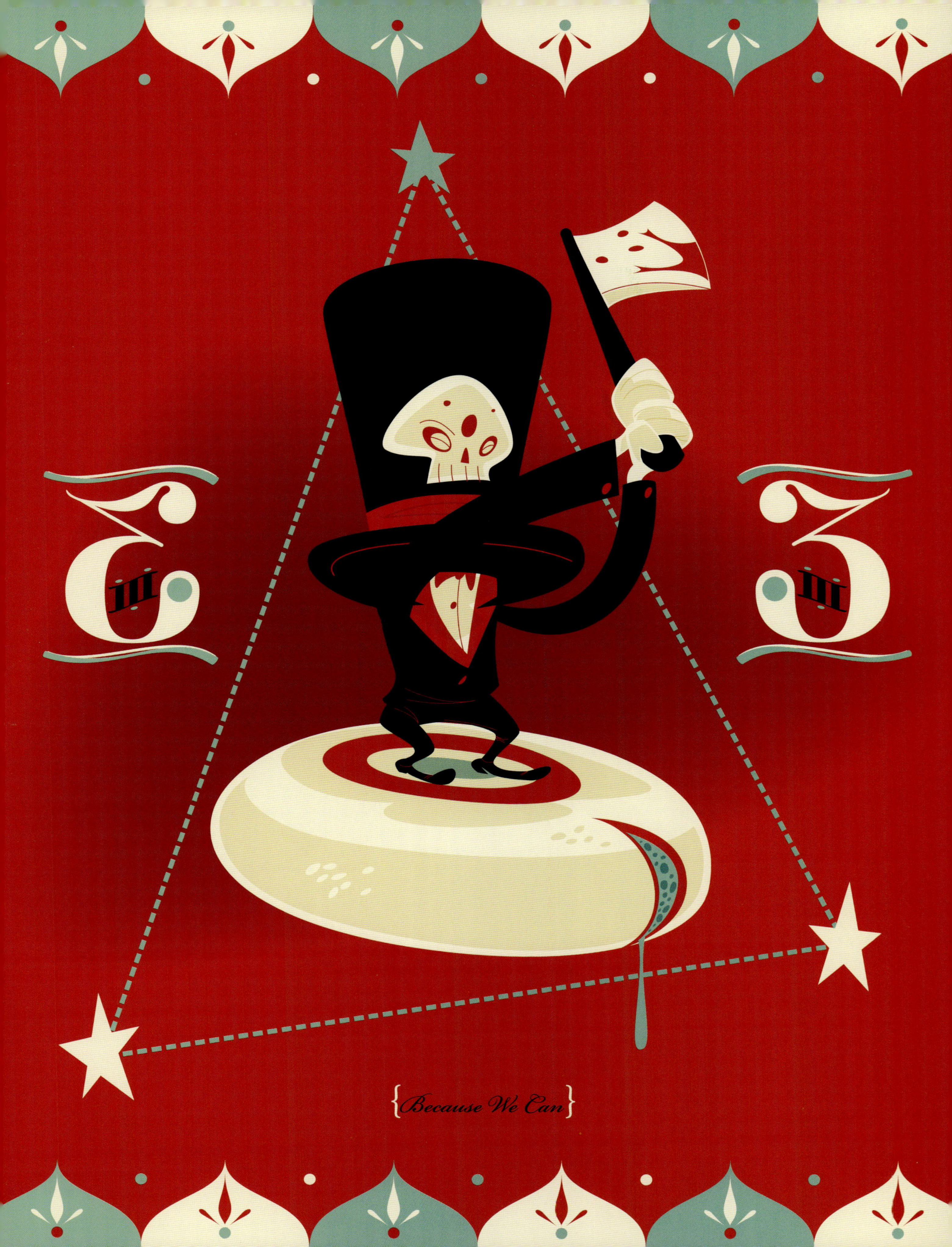
{Because We Can}

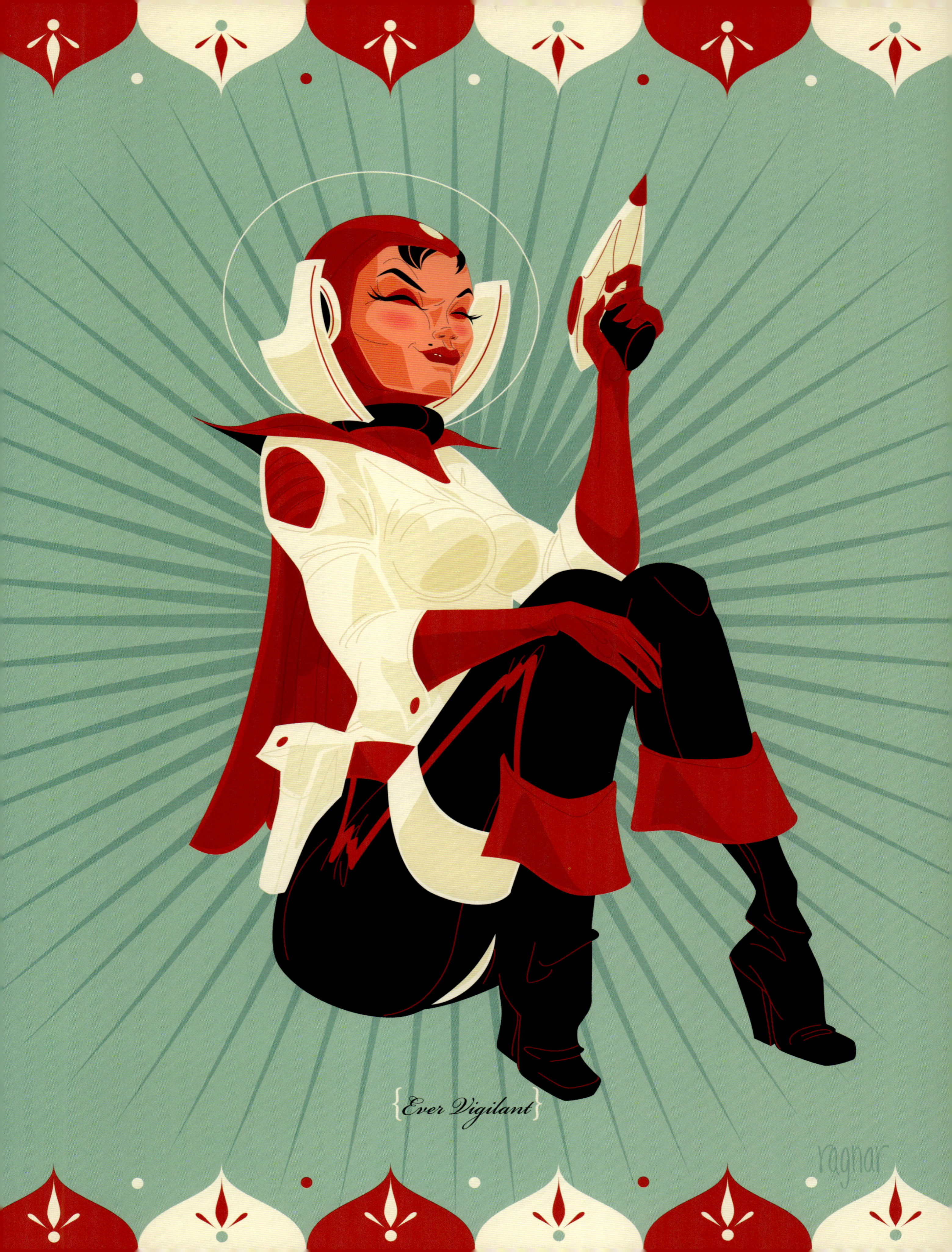
{Ever Vigilant}
ragnar

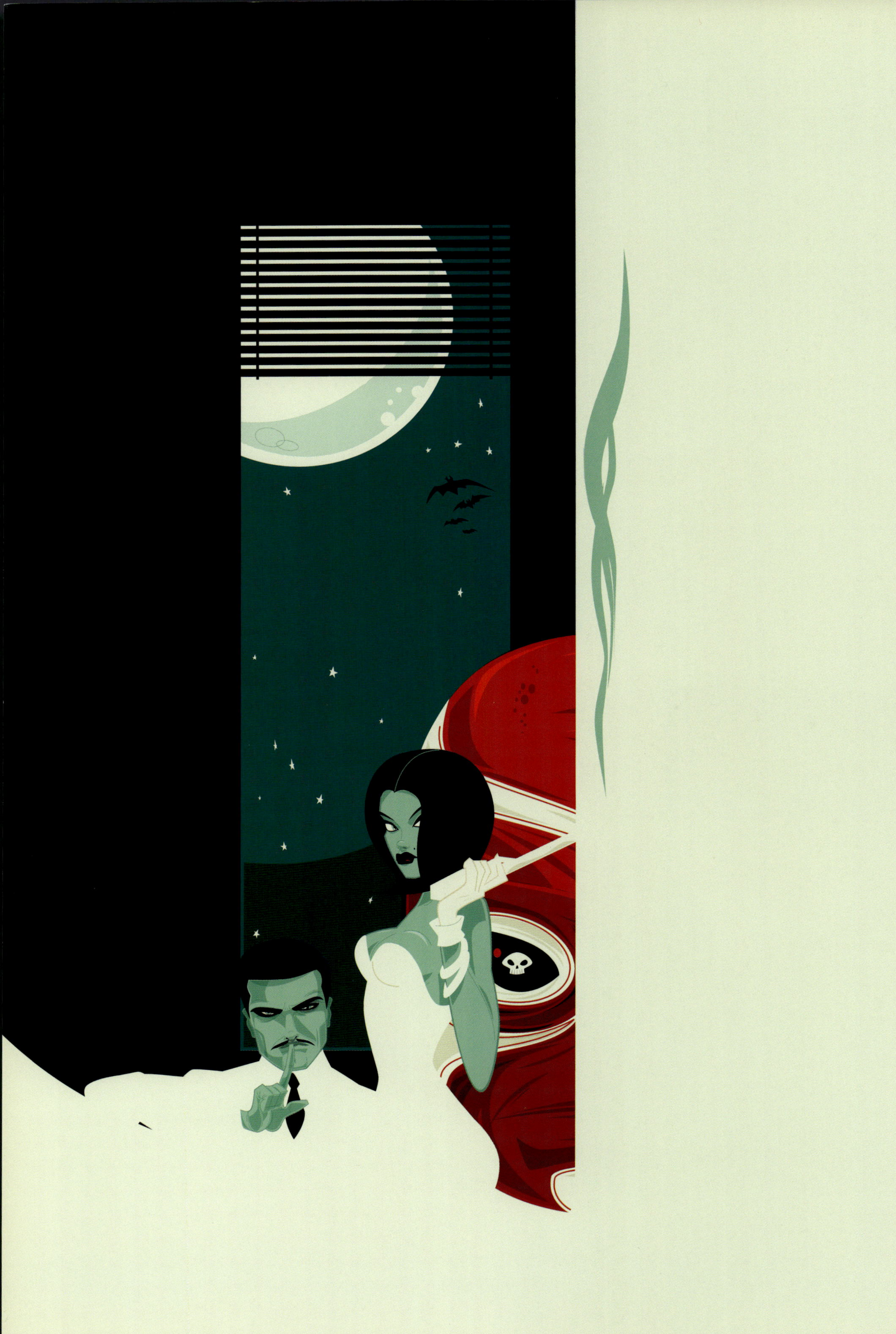

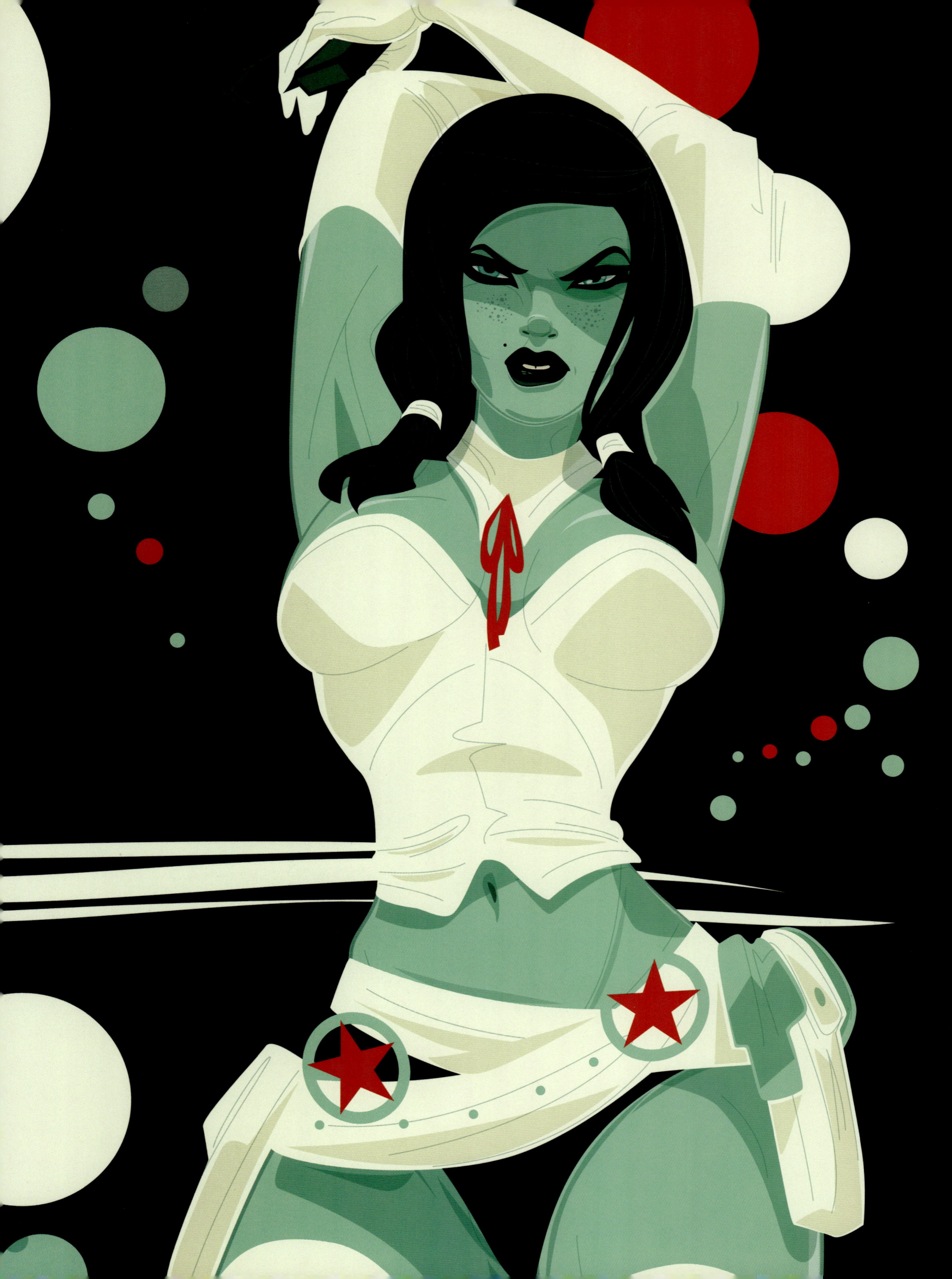

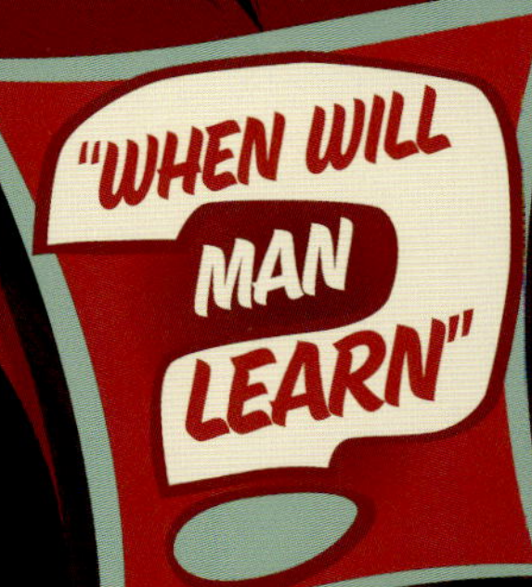

"WHEN WILL MAN LEARN?"

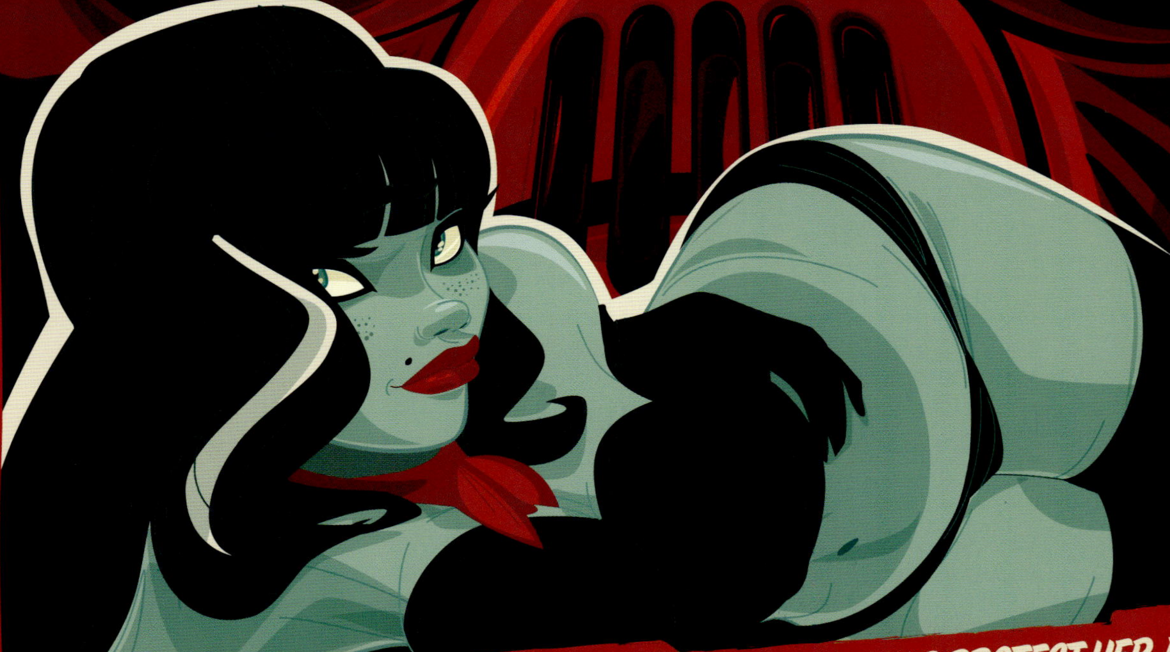

BRI Presents:
"A SHOCKING peek into a world of TORMENT and TERROR!"
STARRING Howard C CARTER
AND Joshua HAMON
CREATED TO BE HER PROTECTOR ... WHO WOULD PROTECT HER FROM...
The "BAD ROBOT"
ragnar
DISTRIBUTED BY
BR
BAD ROBOT INTERNATIONAL
CONSIDER YOURSELF WARNED - MODERN SCIENCE RUNS AMOK - THIS SUMMER!
Filmed entirely in spectacular ROBOCOLOR

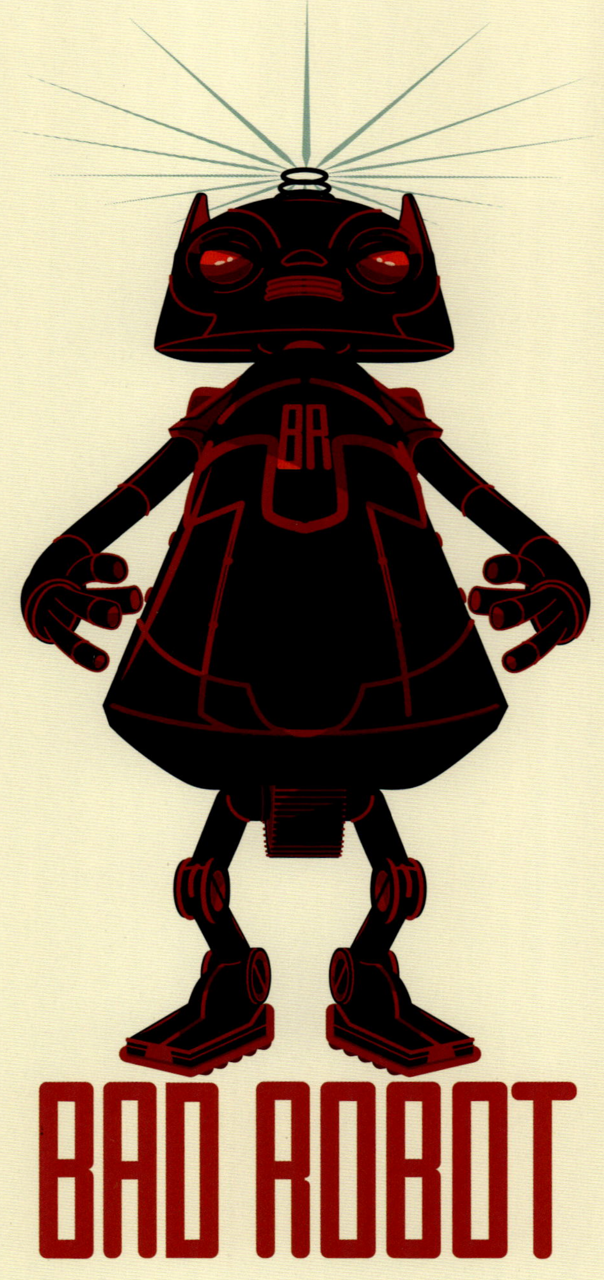

BAD ROBOT

I like my robots with some clunk to 'em. So when I was asked

to do some posters with the clunky, chunky robot that is the

mascot for Bad Robot how could I possibly say no? Well, I

didn't. Say no, that is. I had a good place to start but was also

given free reign to modify and tweak the existing design. So I

did. Tweak it, that is.

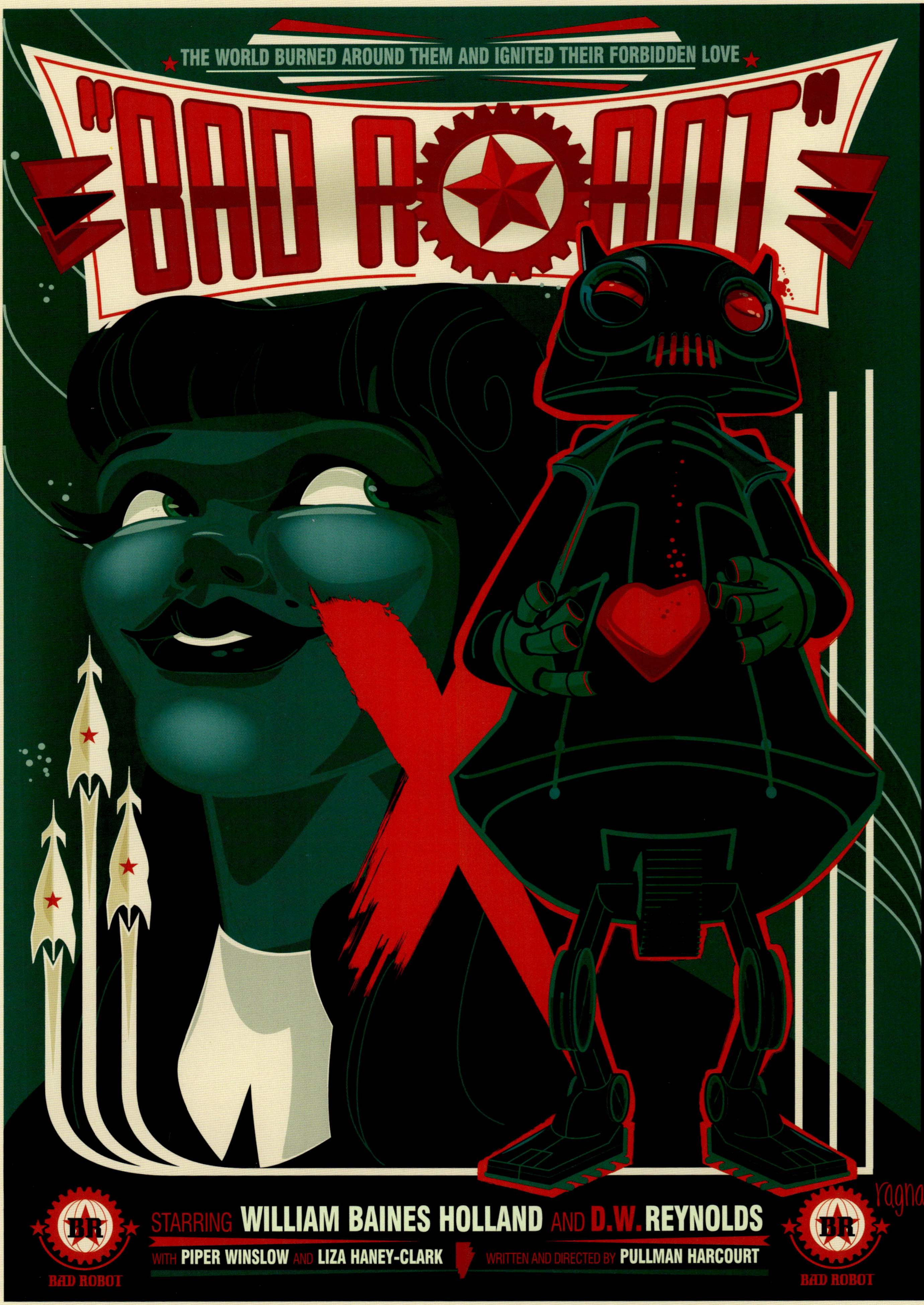

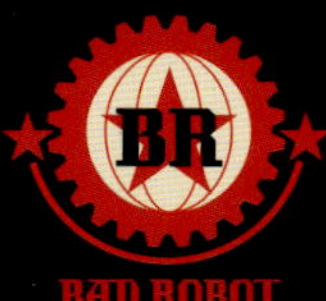
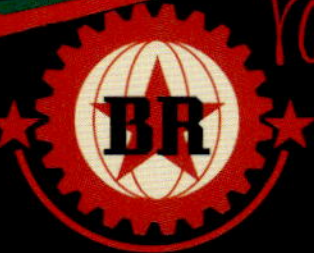

THE WORLD BURNED AROUND THEM AND IGNITED THEIR FORBIDDEN LOVE
"BAD ROBOT"
STARRING WILLIAM BAINES HOLLAND AND D.W. REYNOLDS
WITH PIPER WINSLOW AND LIZA HANEY-CLARK
WRITTEN AND DIRECTED BY PULLMAN HARCOURT
BR
BAD ROBOT
BR
BAD ROBOT
ragnar
© 2007 Bad Robot IP LLC

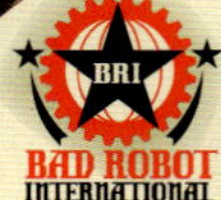

METAL MEN... OUT OF THIS WORLD,
OUT OF CONTROL AND OUT FOR BLOOD!

No WEAPON
Could STOP THEM!
No SIN
Could TEMPT THEM!
Until They
Encountered...
HER!

BAD ROBOT

STARRING PIPER WINSLOW
LIZA HANEY-CLARK

ragnar

BRI
BAD ROBOT
INTERNATIONAL

THIS MOTION PICTURE HAS BEEN FILMED ENTIRELY IN ASTOUNDING ROBOCOLOR FOR THE ULTIMATE CINEMA EXPERIENCE

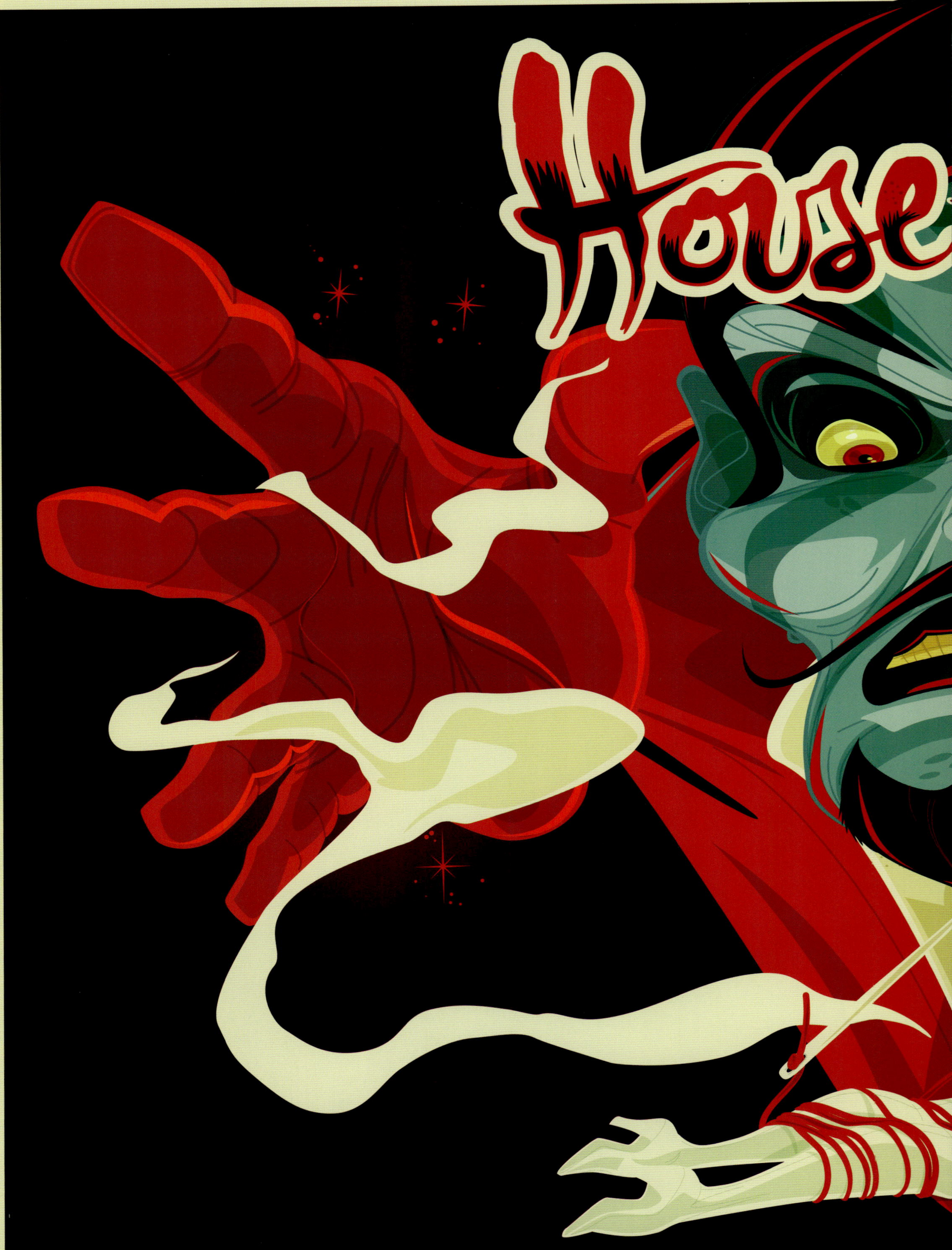
House

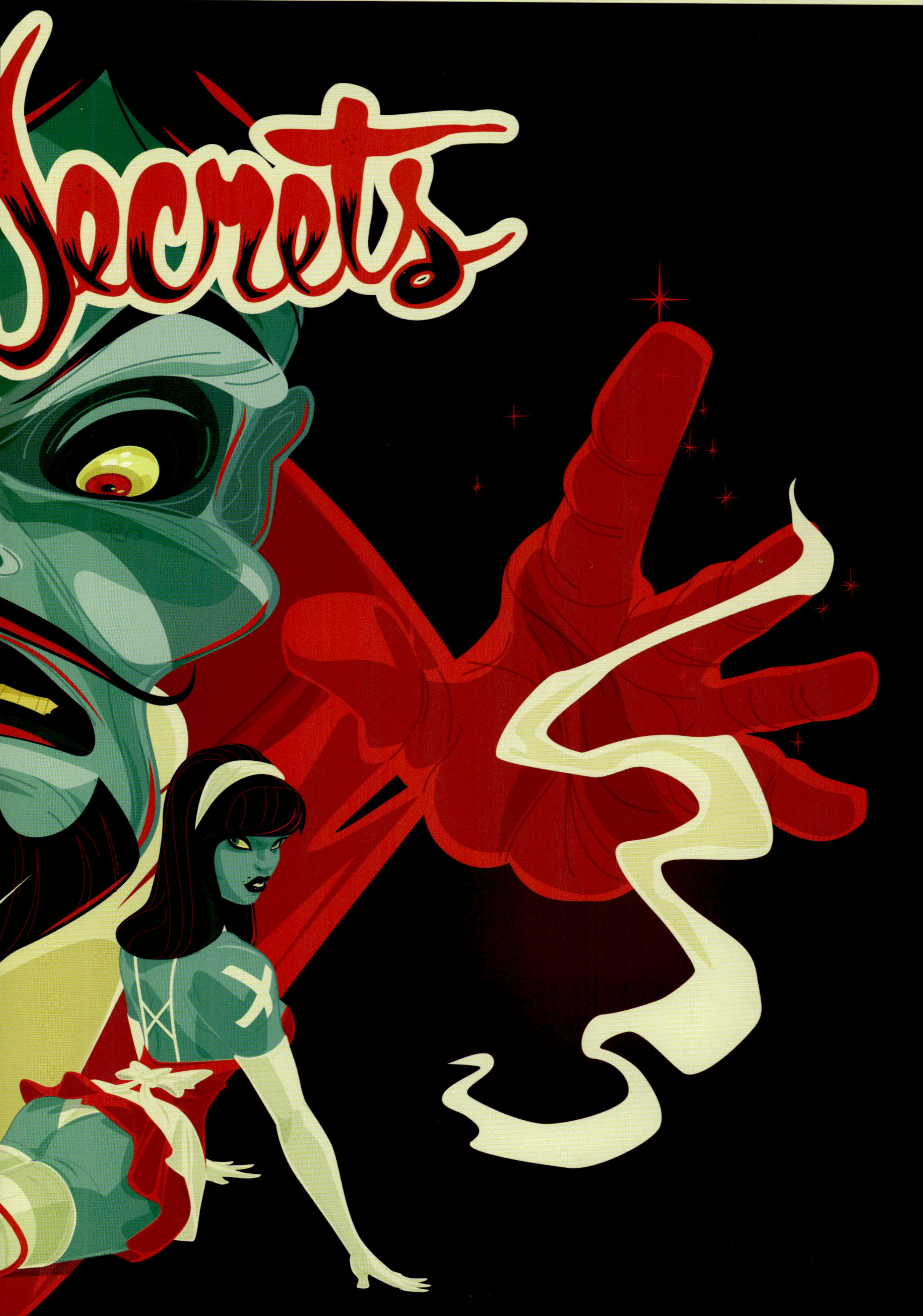
Secrets
ragnar

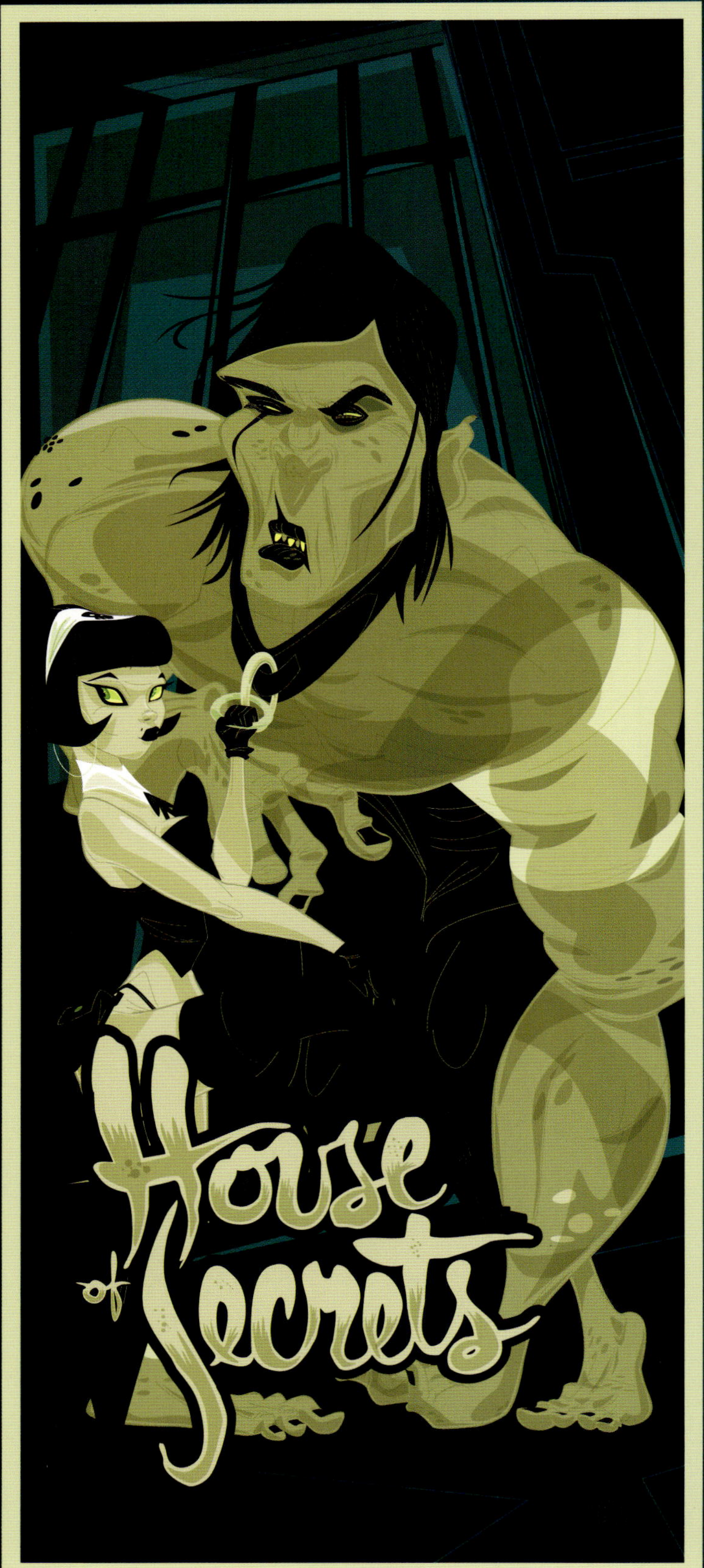

House
of
Secrets
House 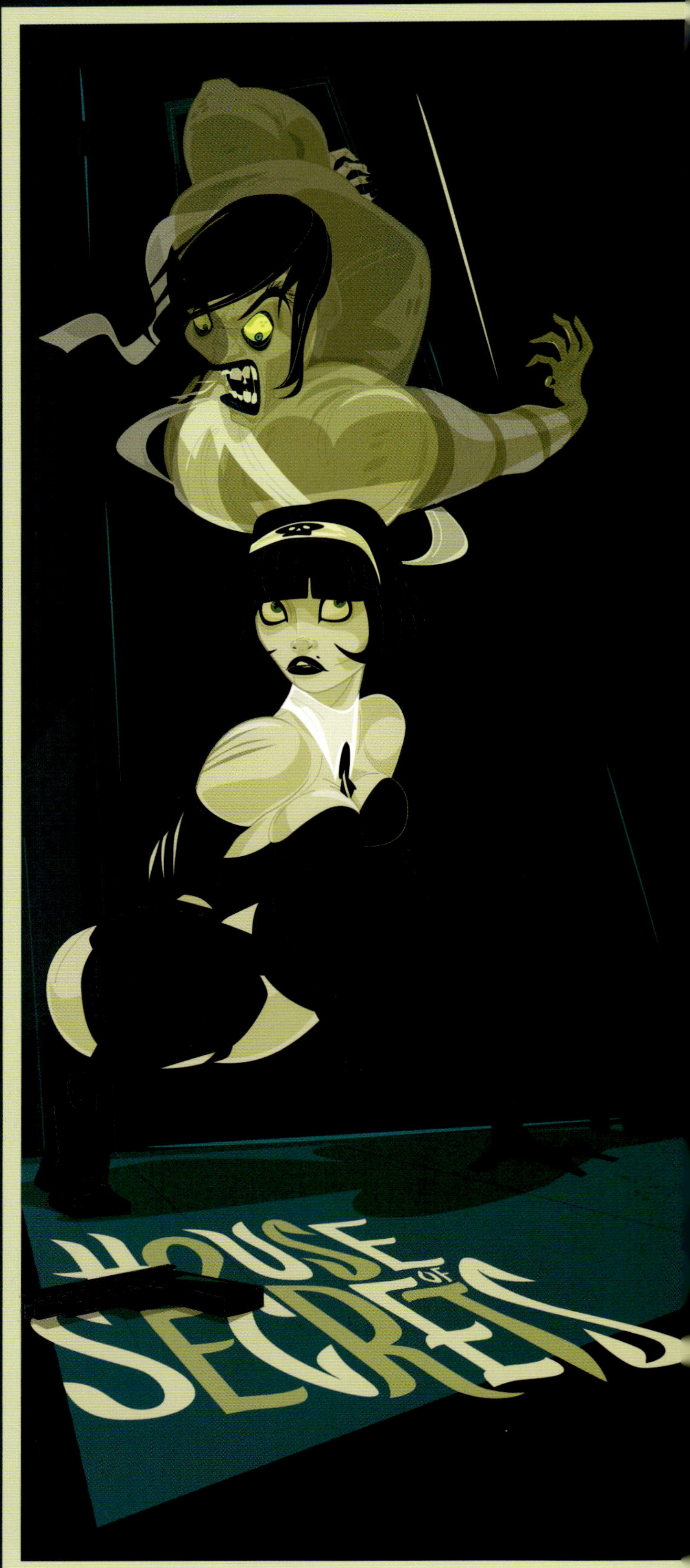
of
SECRETS

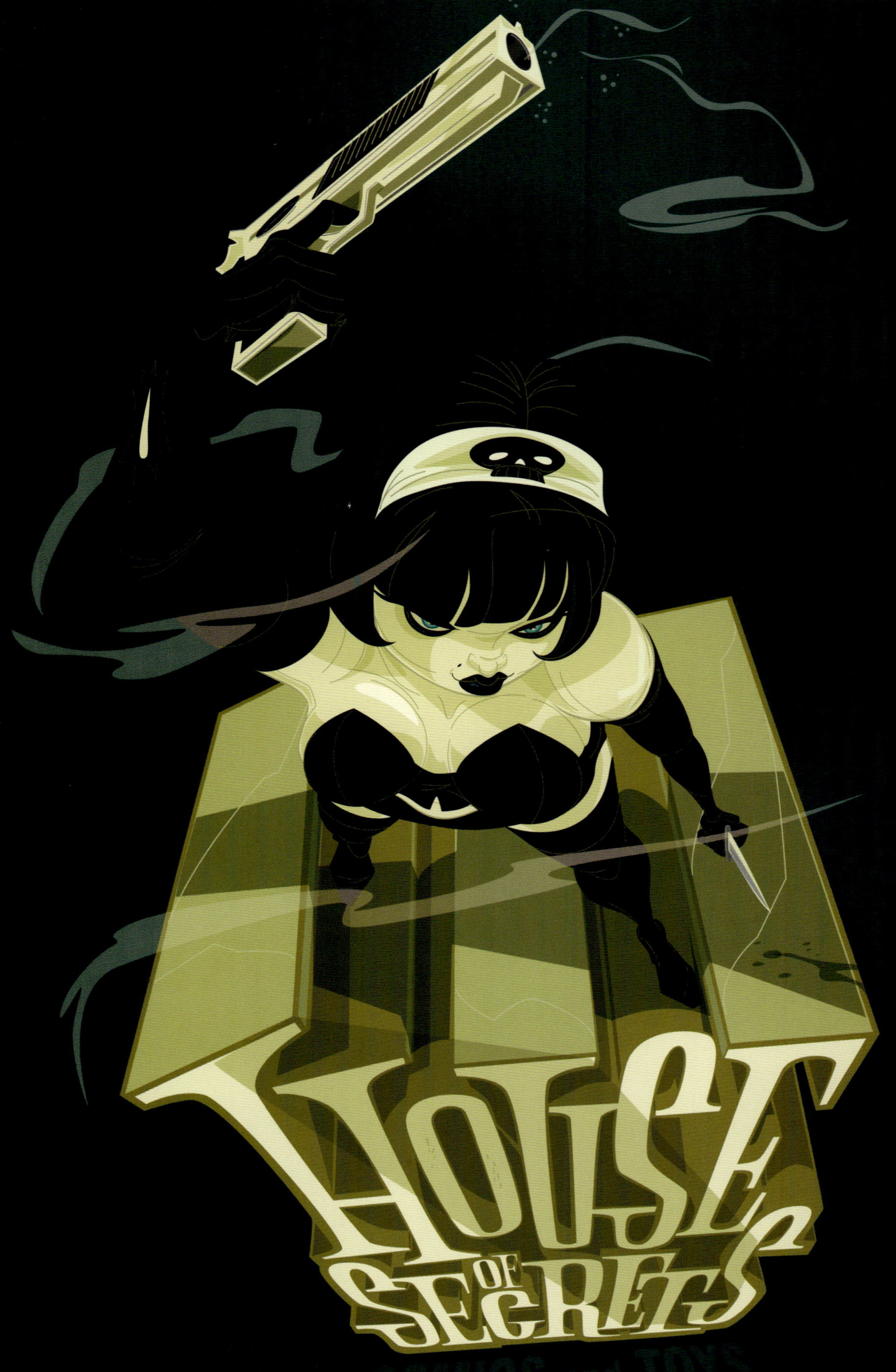

HOUSE
OF
SECRETS
COMICS and TOYS

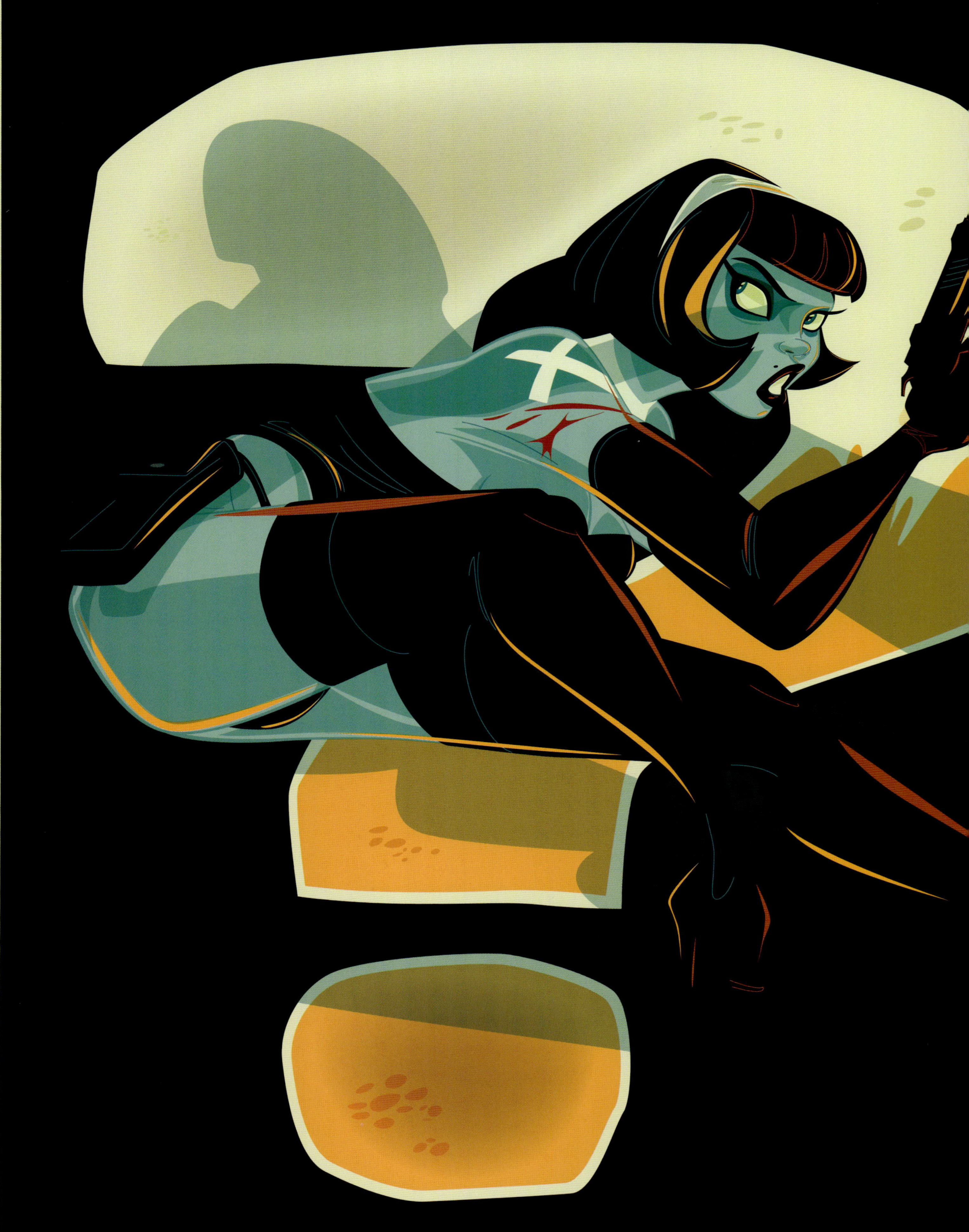

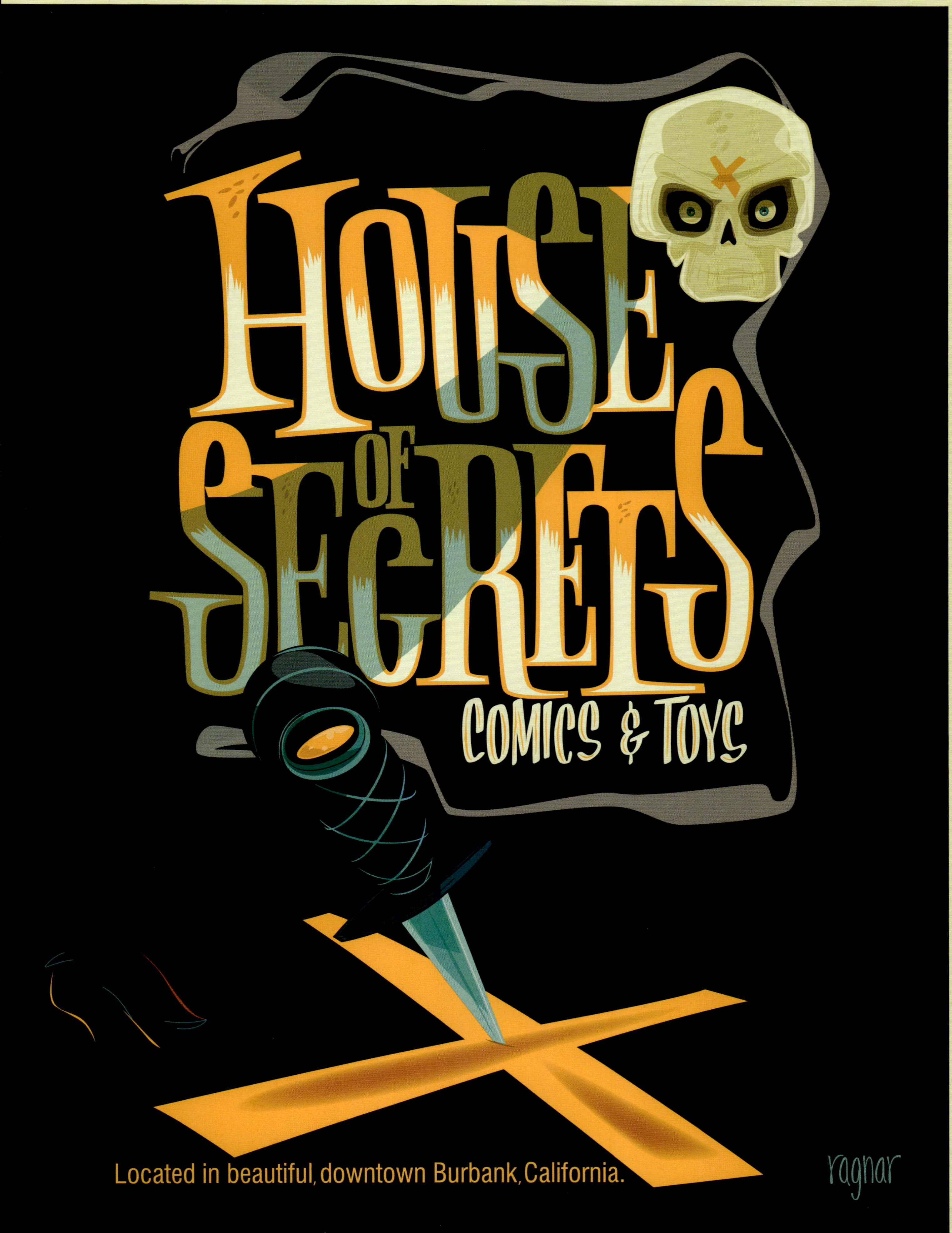

House
of
Secrets
Comics & Toys
Located in beautiful, downtown Burbank, California.
ragnar

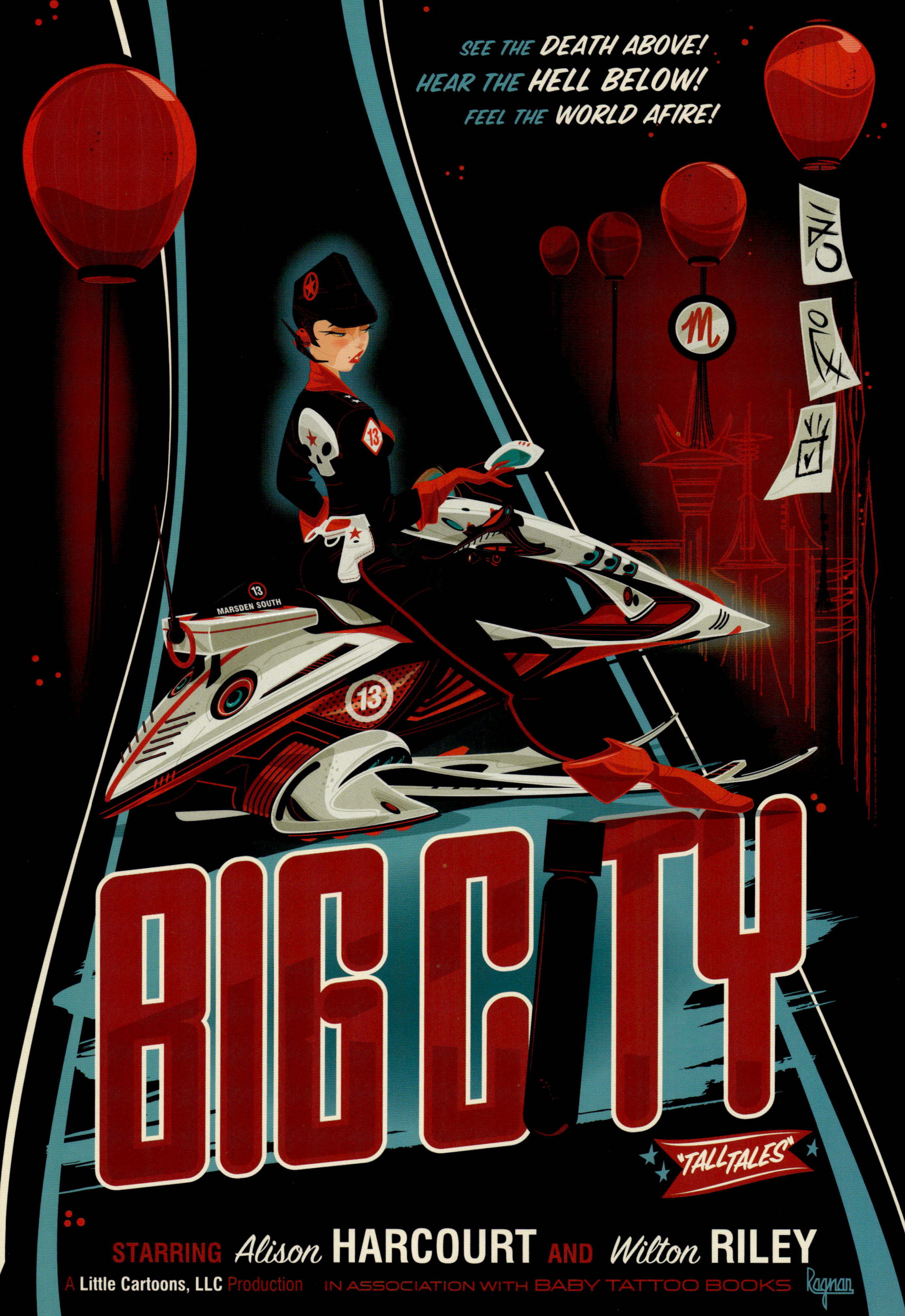

SEE THE DEATH ABOVE!
HEAR THE HELL BELOW!
FEEL THE WORLD AFIRE!
MARSDEN SOUTH
13
BIG CITY
"TALL TALES"
STARRING Alison HARCOURT AND Wilton RILEY
A Little Cartoons, LLC Production   IN ASSOCIATION WITH BABY TATTOO BOOKS
Ragnar

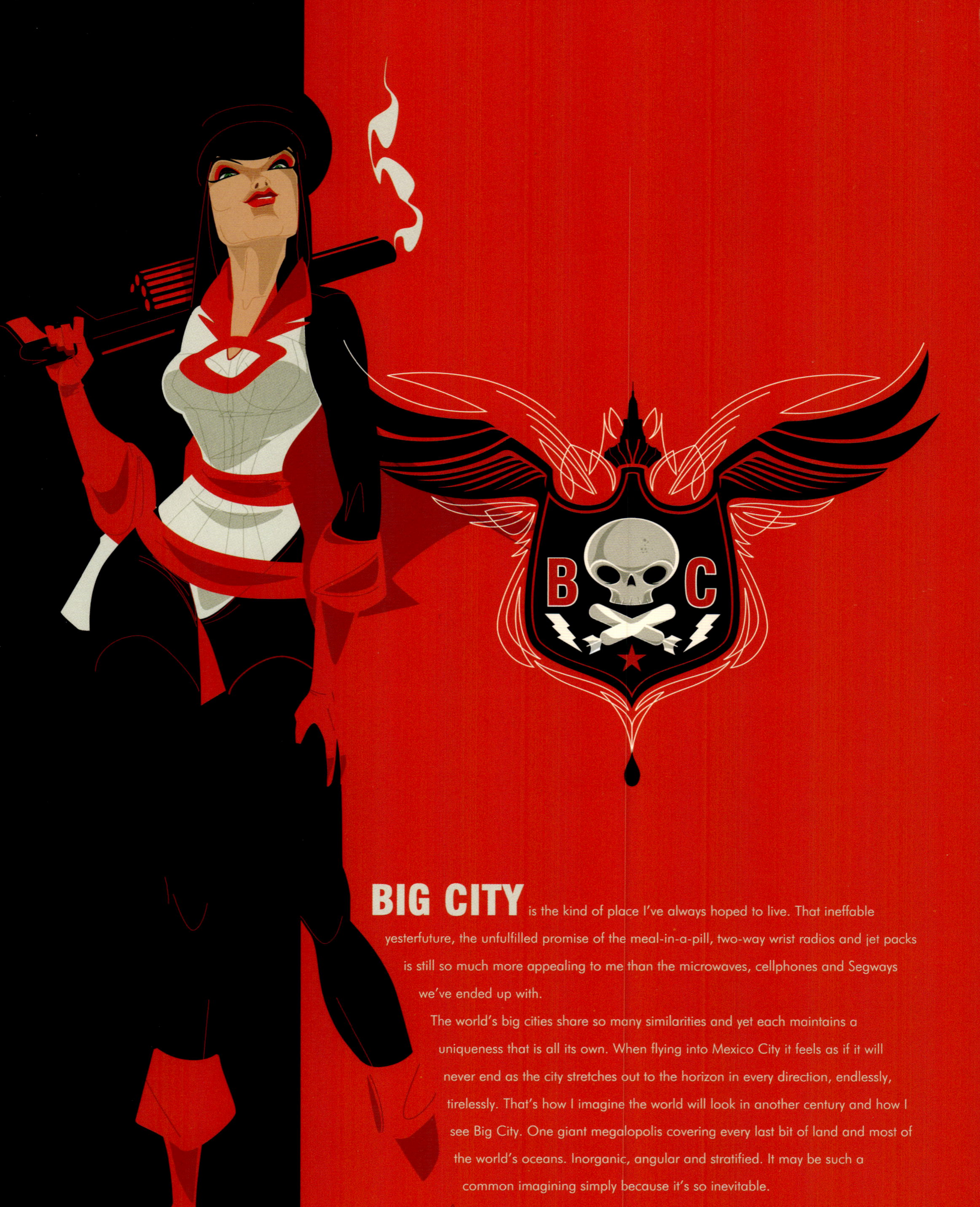

BIG CITY is the kind of place I've always hoped to live. That ineffable yesterfuture, the unfulfilled promise of the meal-in-a-pill, two-way wrist radios and jet packs is still so much more appealing to me than the microwaves, cellphones and Segways we've ended up with.

The world's big cities share so many similarities and yet each maintains a uniqueness that is all its own. When flying into Mexico City it feels as if it will never end as the city stretches out to the horizon in every direction, endlessly, tirelessly. That's how I imagine the world will look in another century and how I see Big City. One giant megalopolis covering every last bit of land and most of the world's oceans. Inorganic, angular and stratified. It may be such a common imagining simply because it's so inevitable.

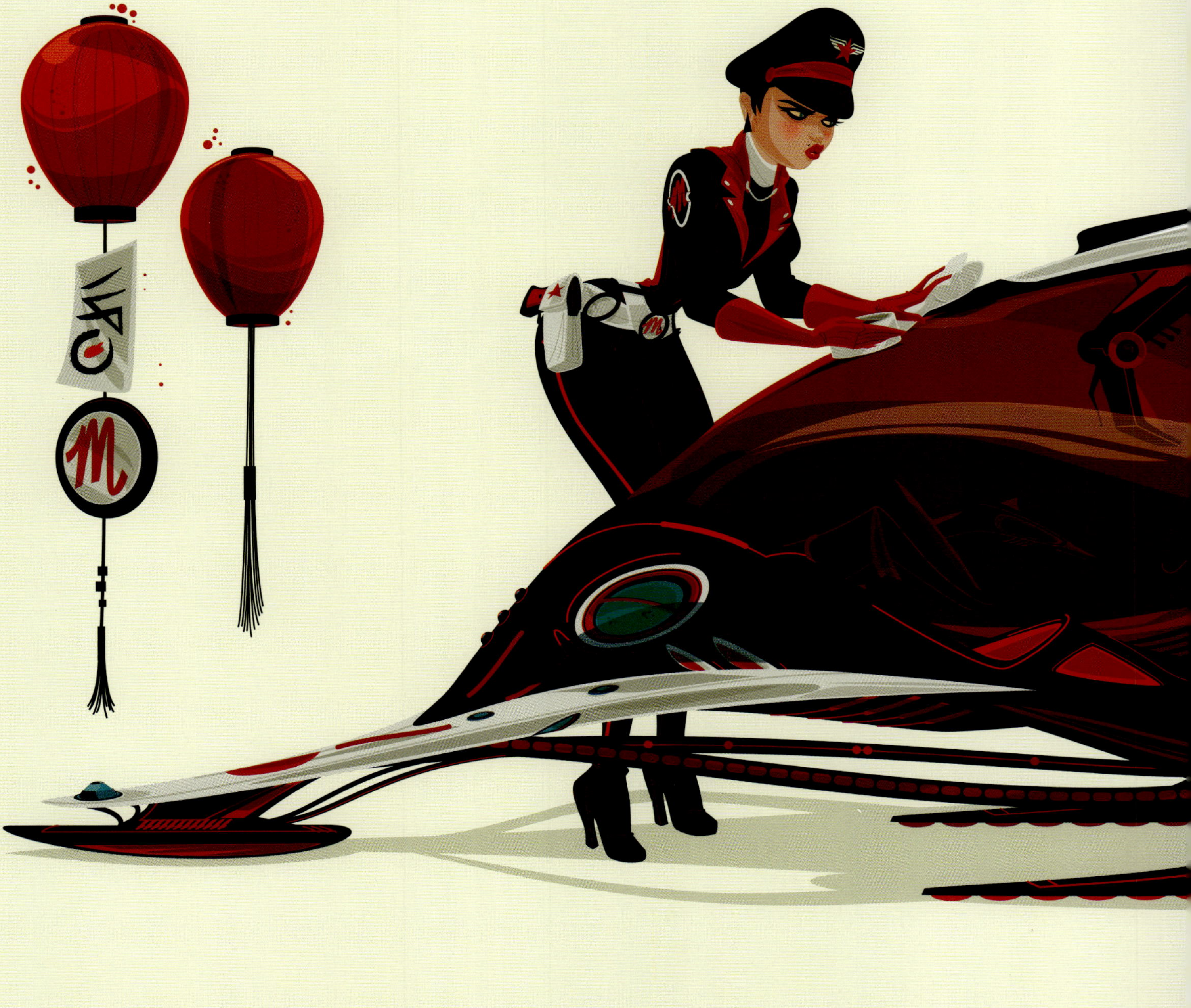

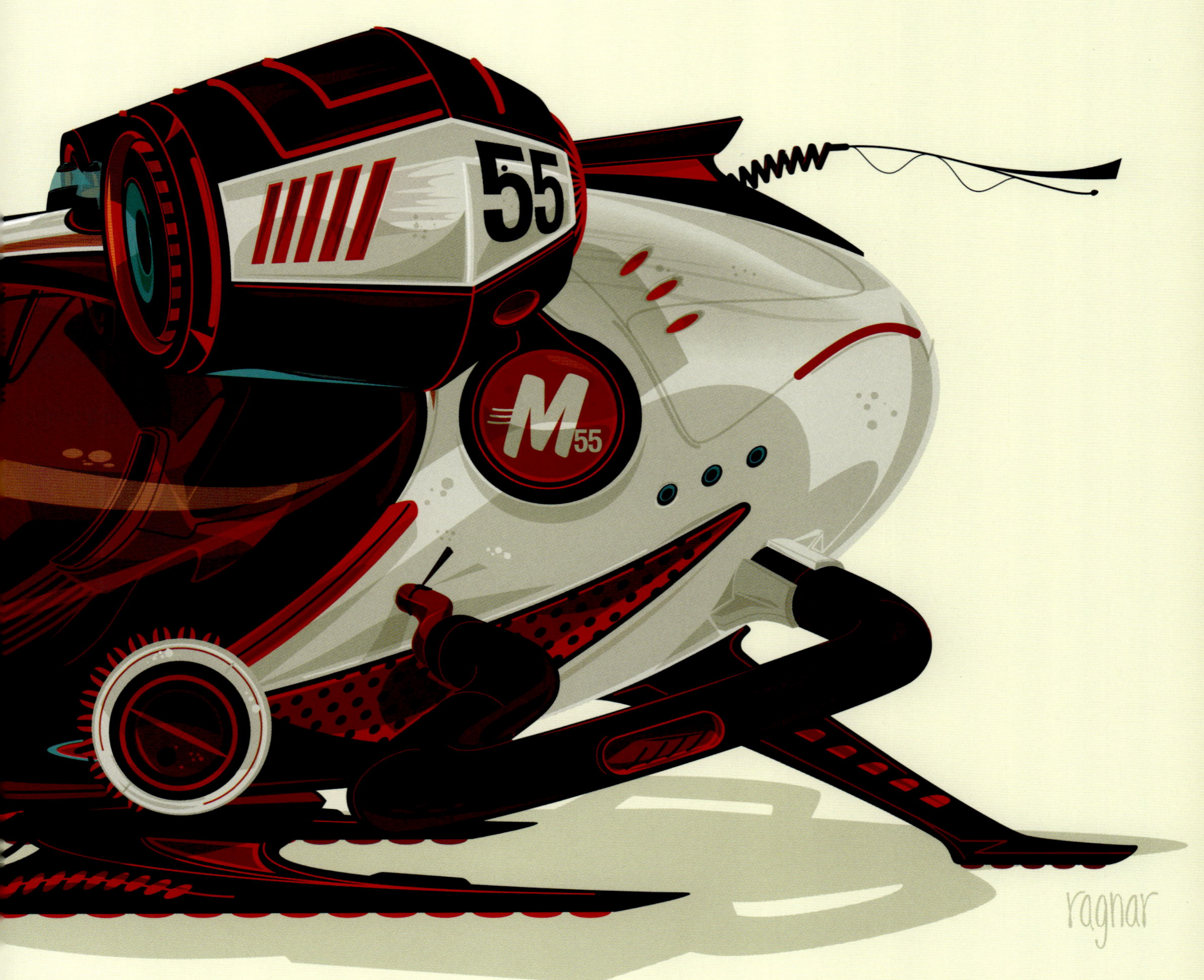
55
M 55
ragnar

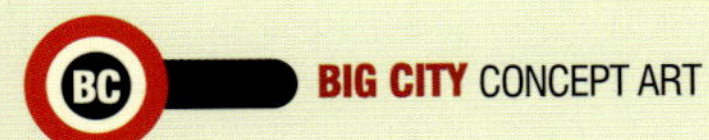BIG CITY CONCEPT ART

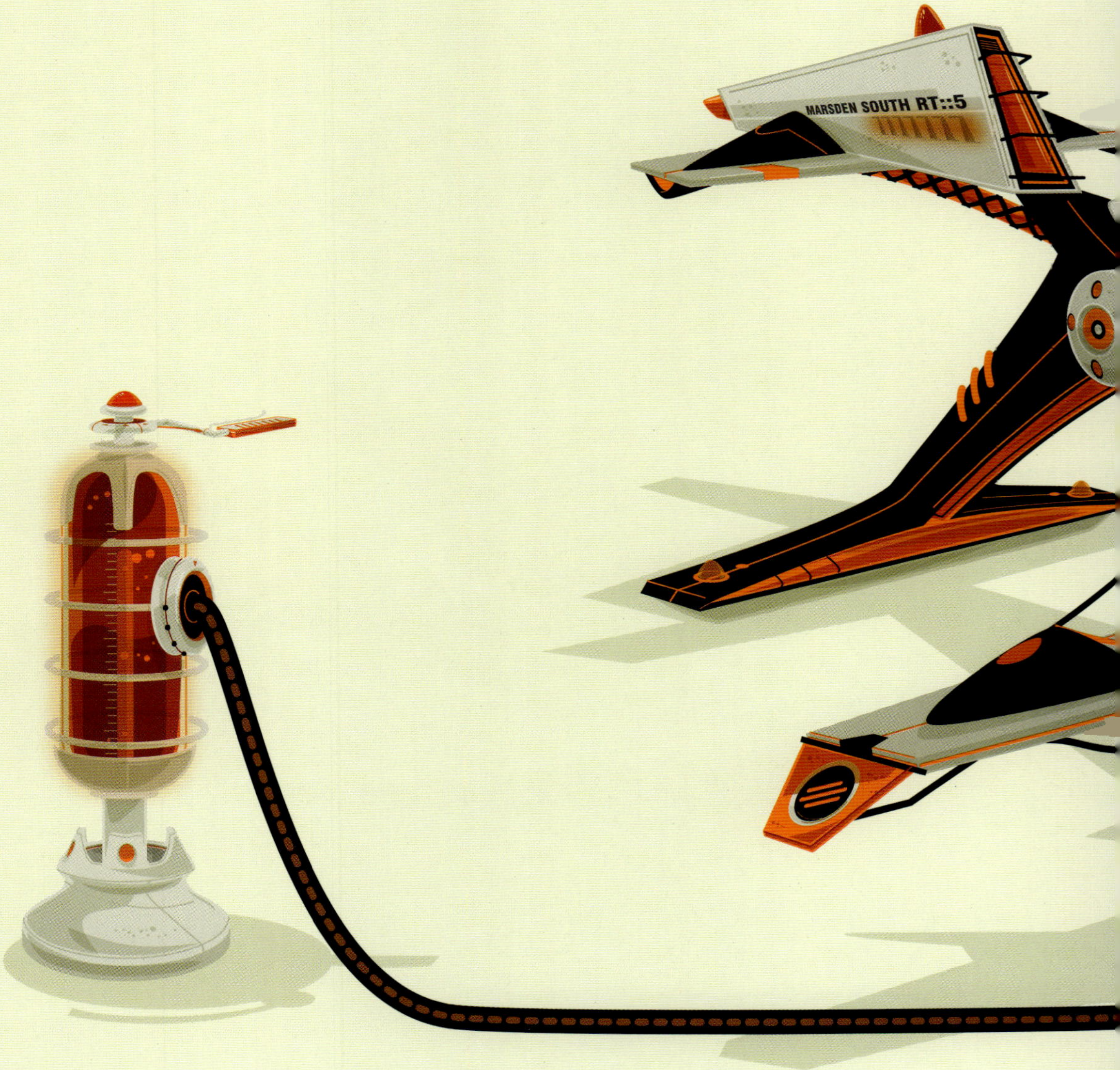

MARSDEN SOUTH RT::5

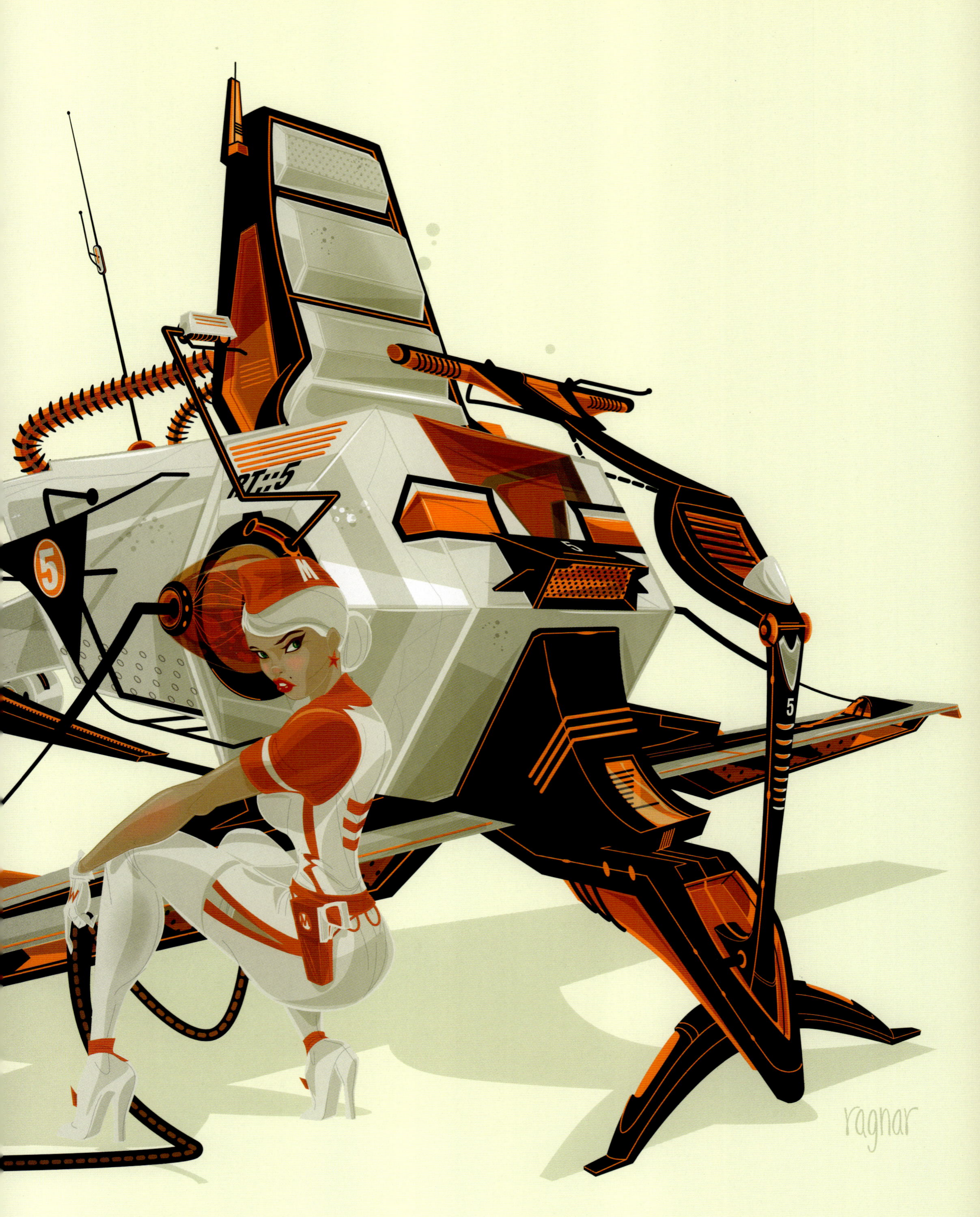
5
ragnar

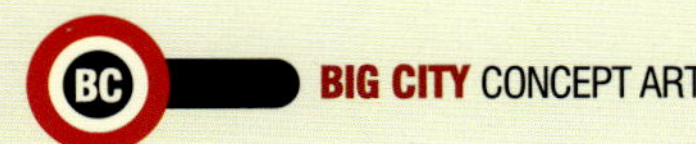

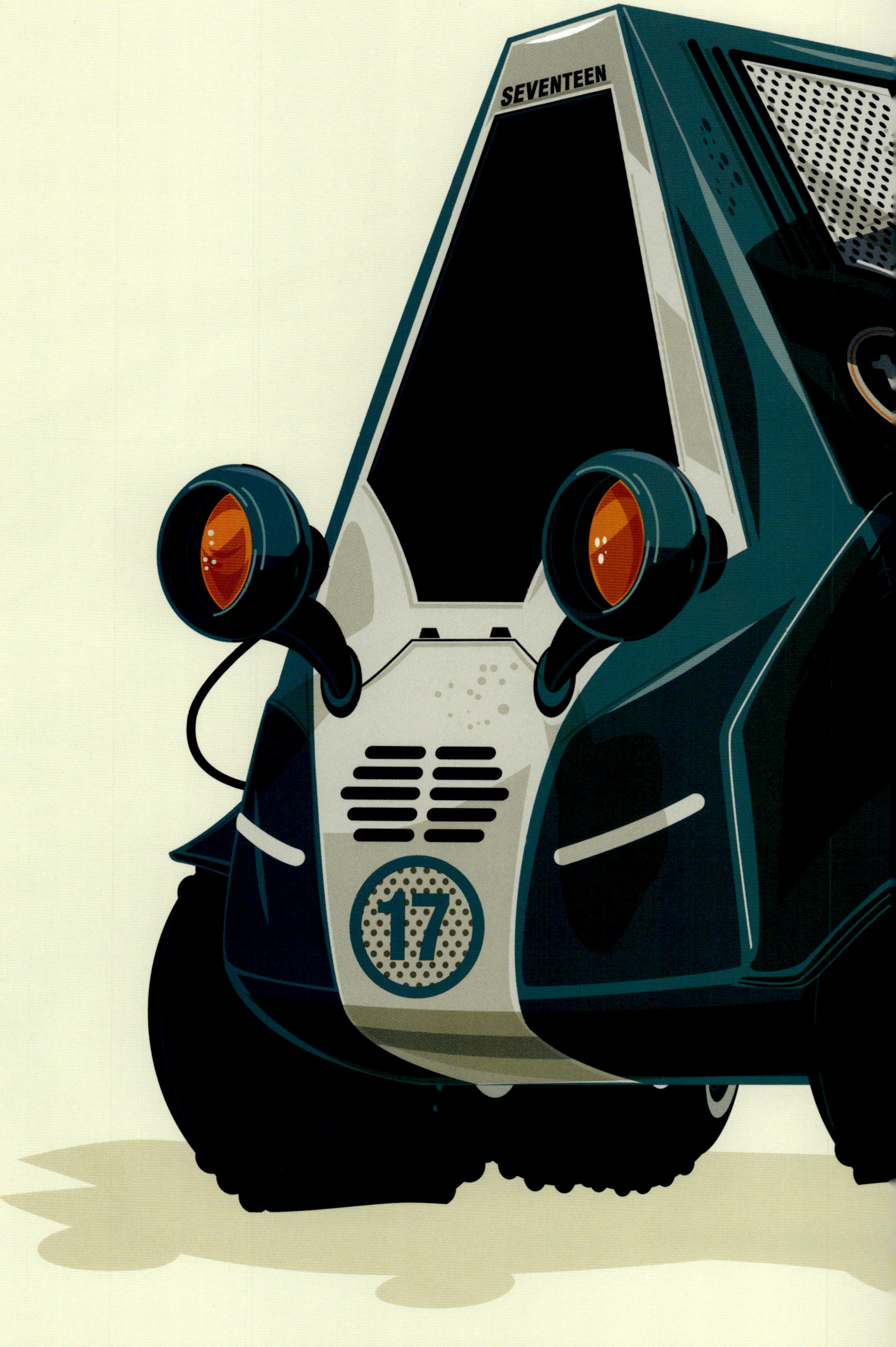

SEVENTEEN
17

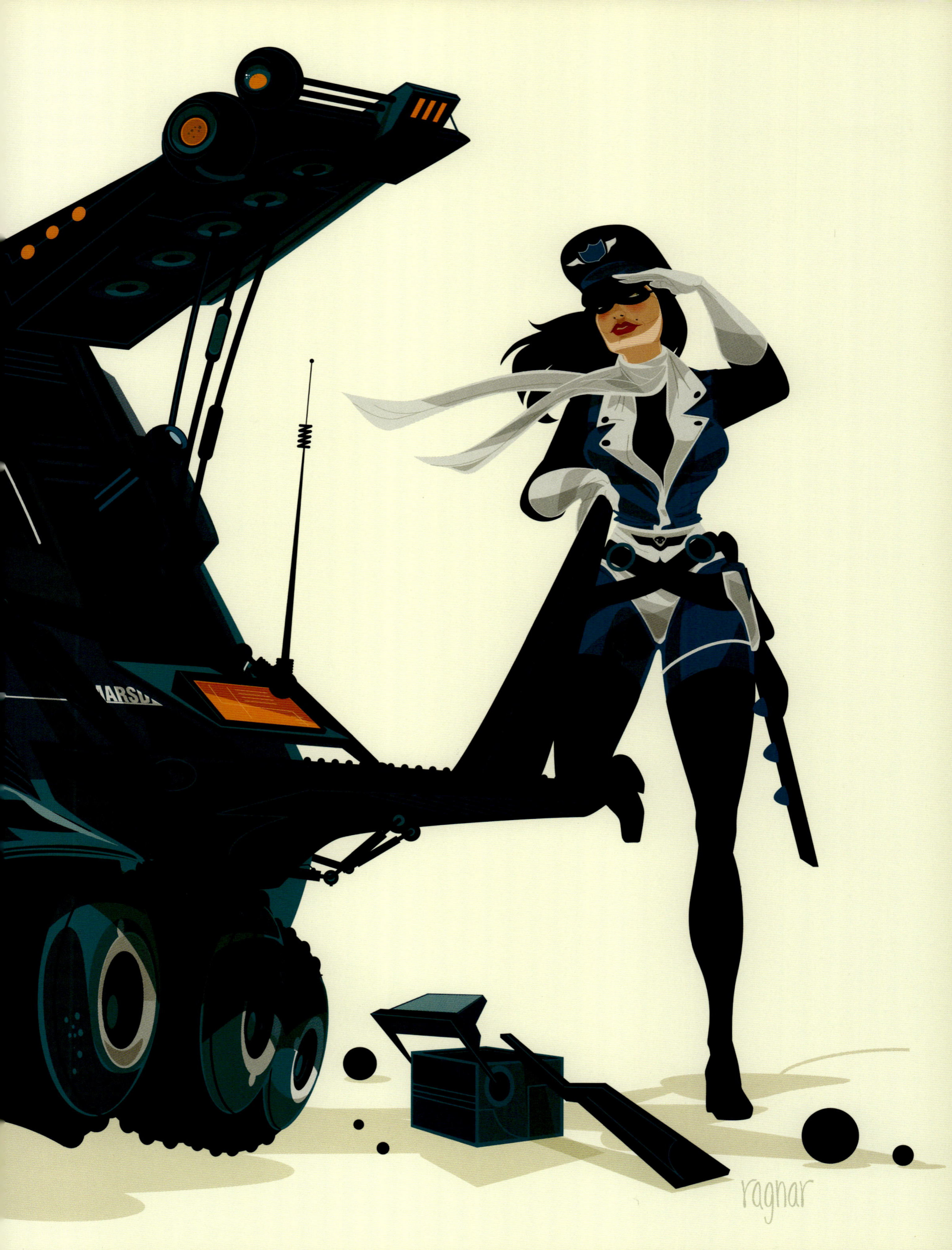

MARSD
ragnar

As is sci-fi tradition, the shapes of the vehicles in Big City are biomimetic. They're forms drawn from the natural world. Insects, animals and plants sheathed in metal, glass and yet to be discovered elements like strongtonium, impervium and unbreakablite. Some traditions should be revered rather than shunned. Though I have tried to steer clear of the most clichéd shapes such as scorpions and spiders.

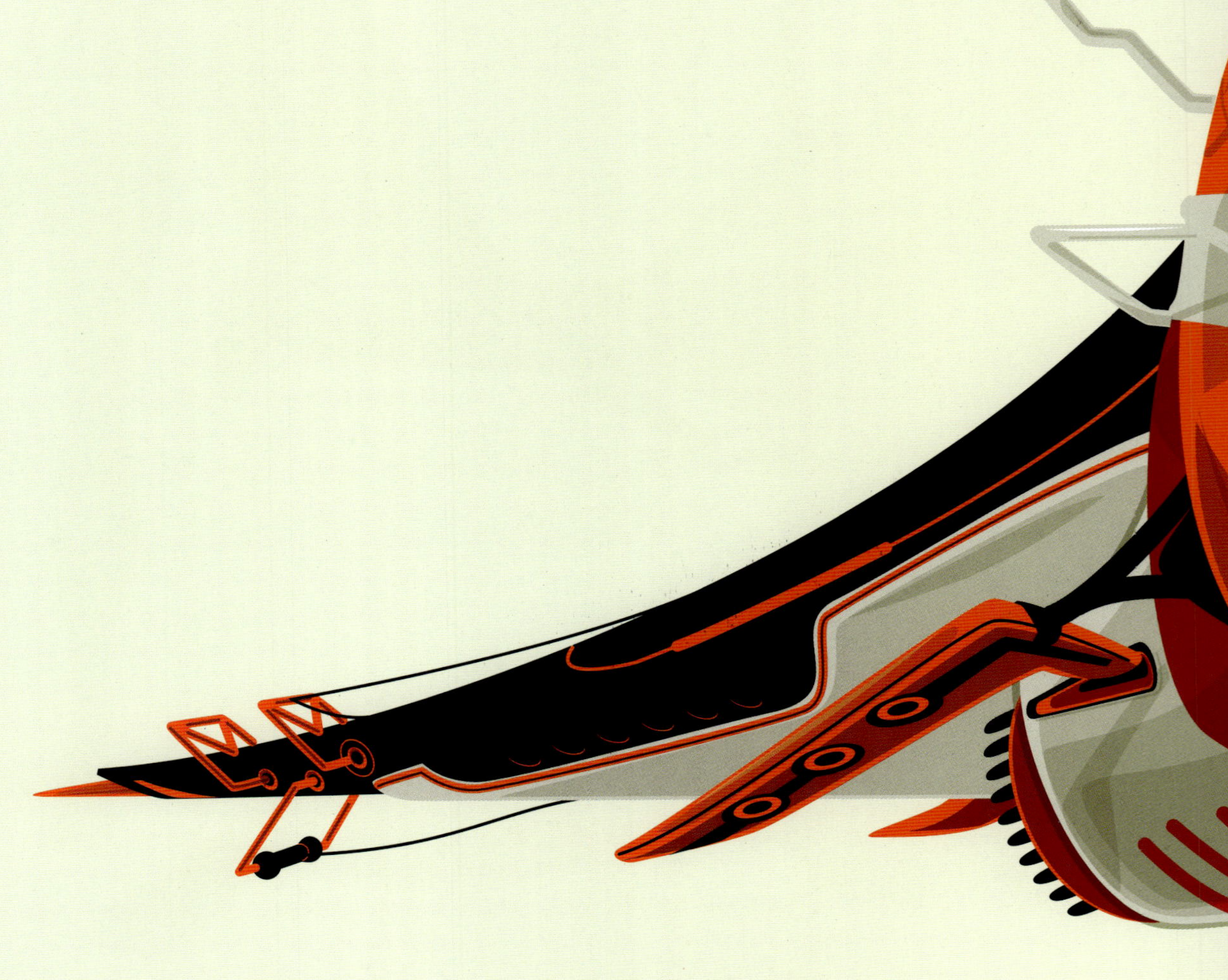

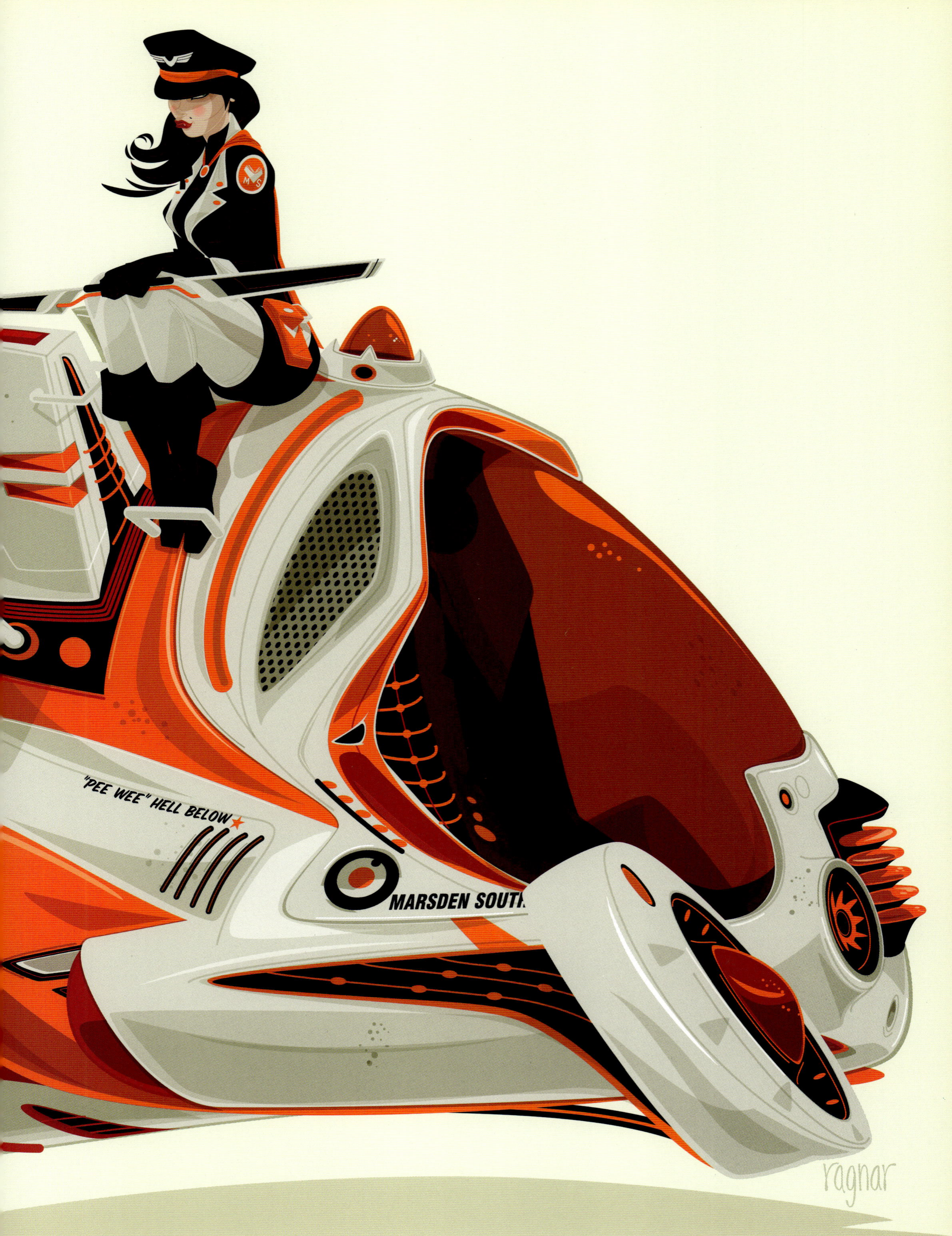

"PEE WEE" HELL BELOW
MARSDEN SOUTH
ragnar

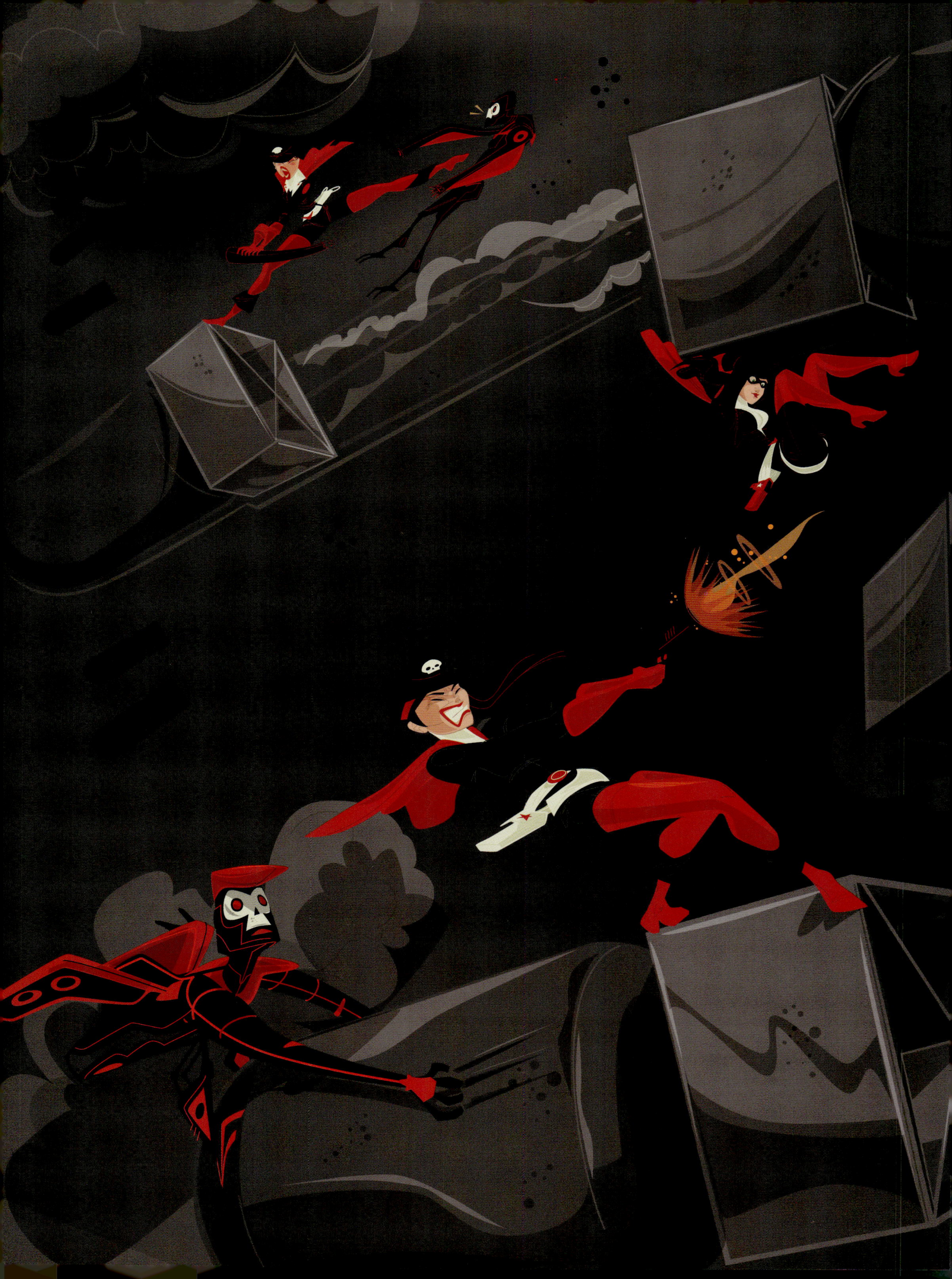

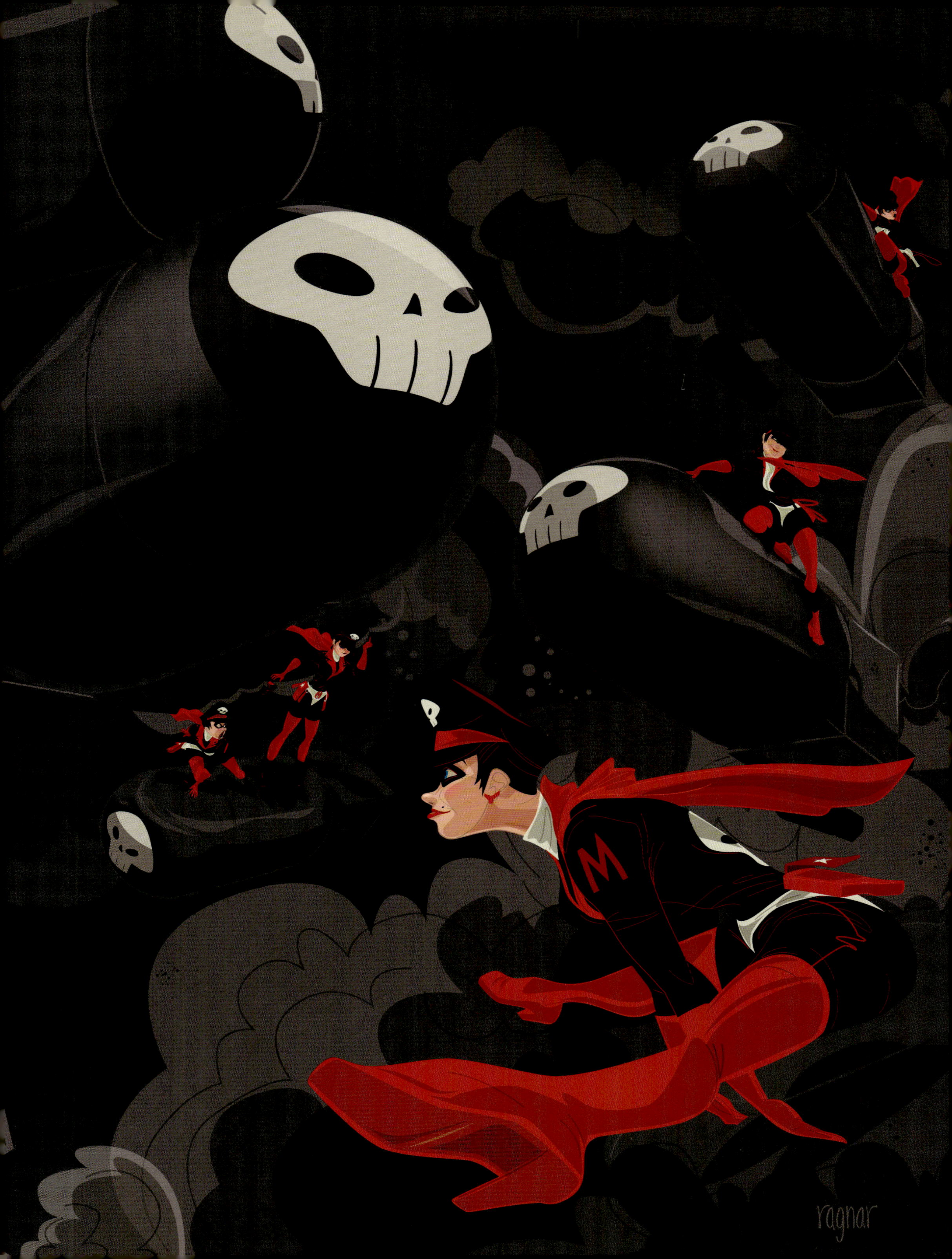

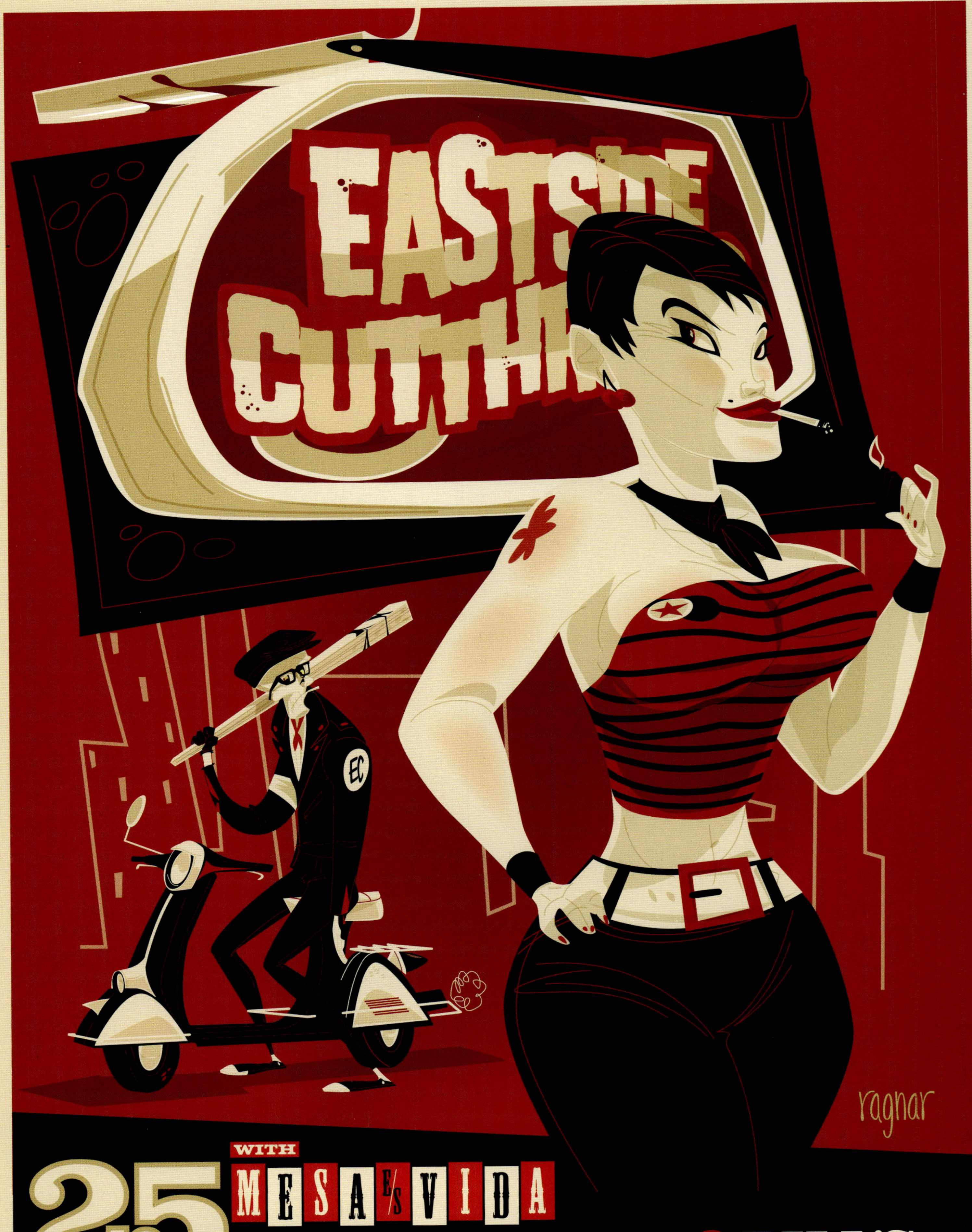

EASTSIDE
CUTHR
EC
ragnar
WITH
25
MESA Es VIDA
SEPTEMBER 9-12 @ BILL'S

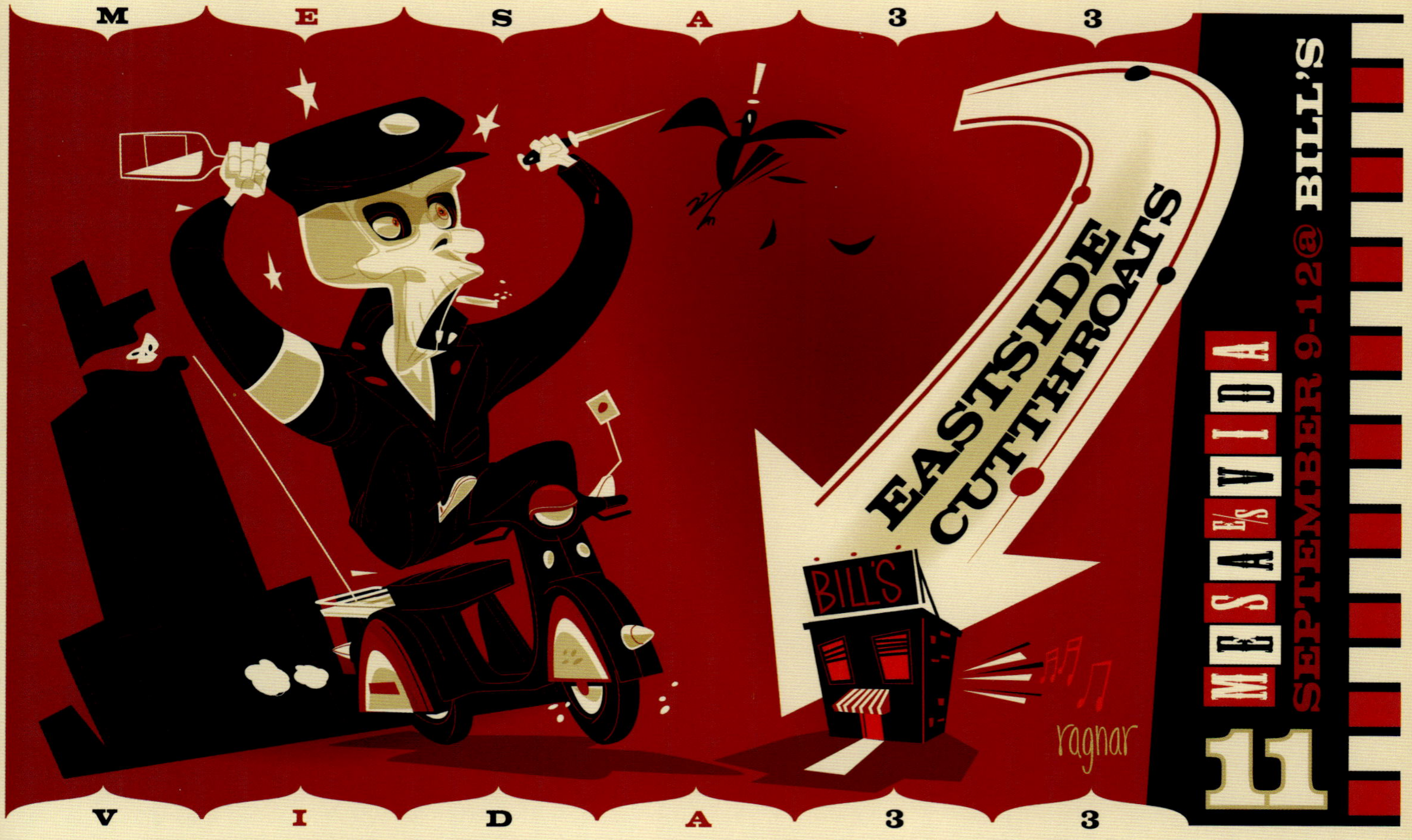

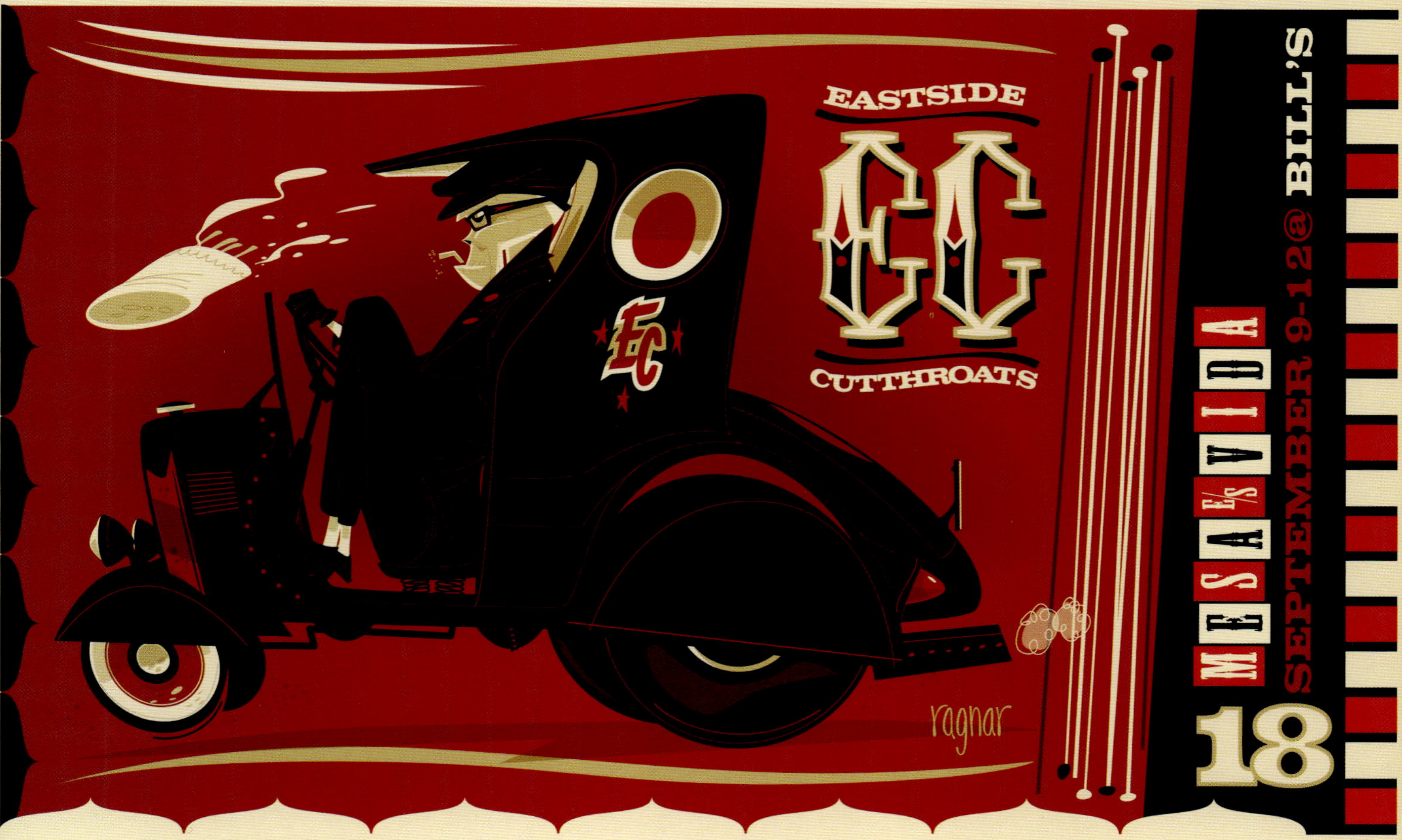

I wish I had the chance to do more gigposters. I have a sincere fondness for them. After all, the first of my illustrations that ever saw print were for flyers for some of my favorite bands. My posters are still littered with the requisite skulls and rock-n-roll iconography, however they'll always feel a bit out of context when not on tattered photocopy paper stuck to the wall with thumbtacks.

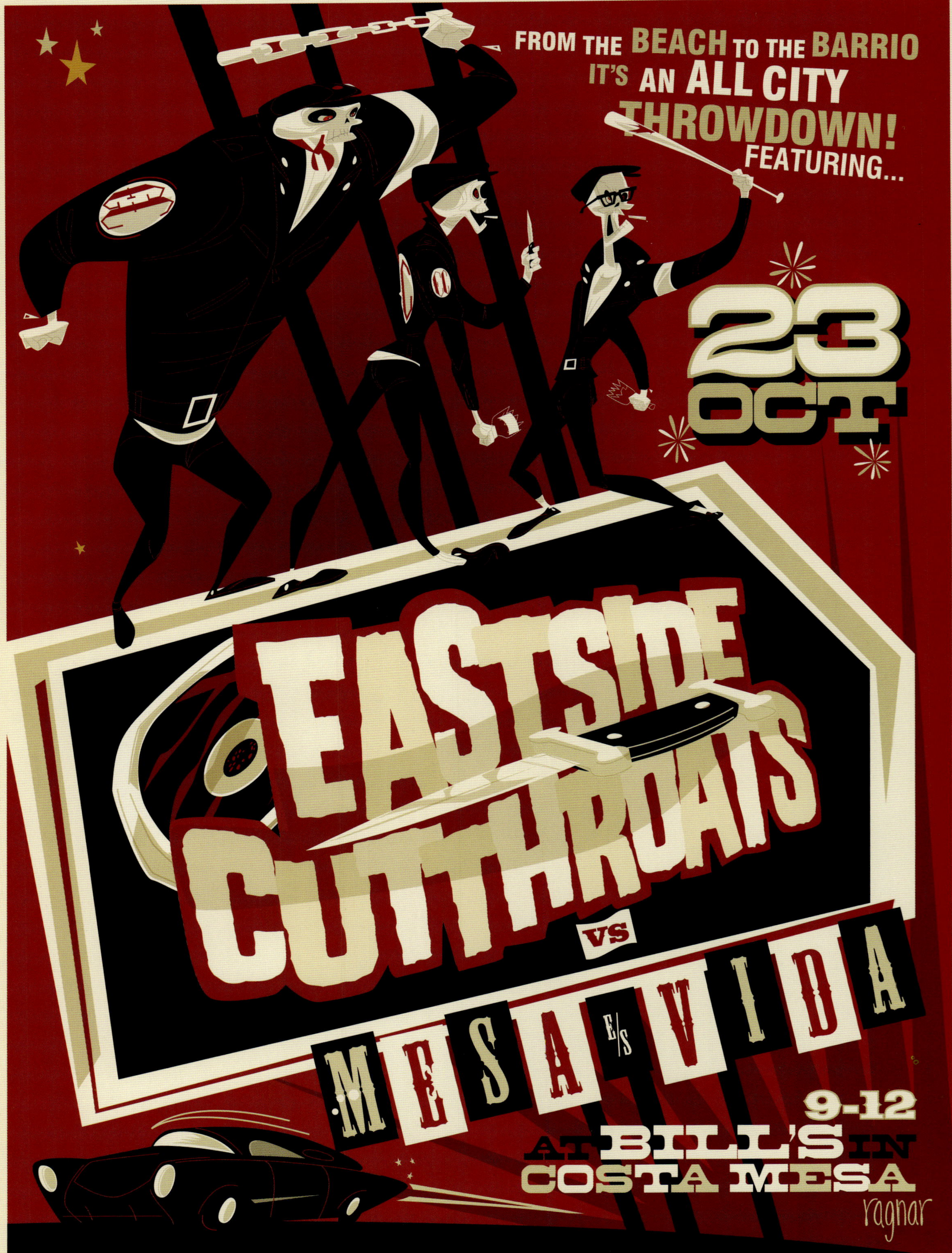

FROM THE BEACH TO THE BARRIO
IT'S AN ALL CITY
THROWDOWN!
FEATURING...
23 OCT
EASTSIDE CUTTHROATS
VS
MESA E/S VIDA
9-12
AT BILL'S IN COSTA MESA
ragnar

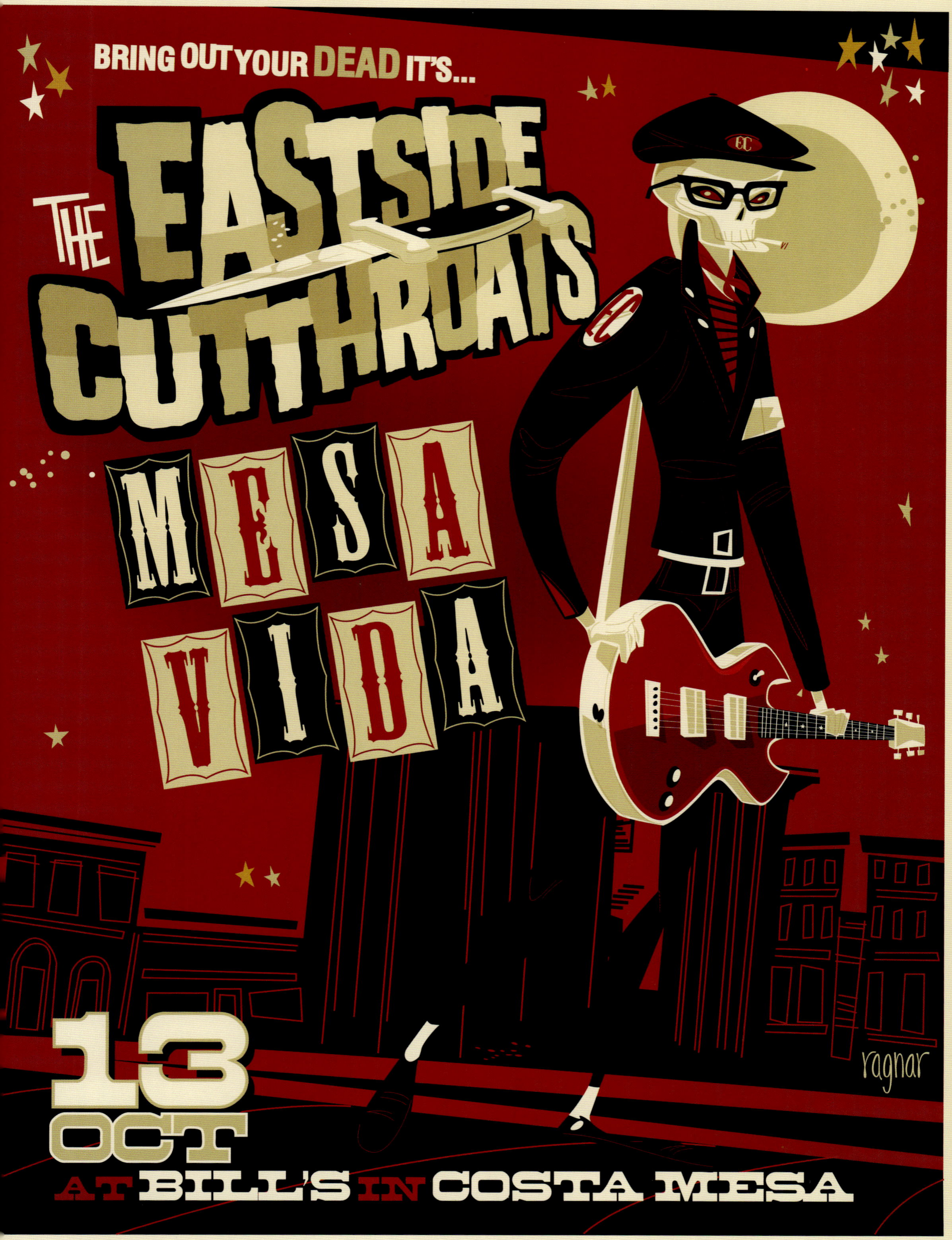

BRING OUT YOUR DEAD IT'S...
THE EASTSIDE CUTTHROATS
MESA VIDA
13 OCT
AT BILL'S IN COSTA MESA
ragnar

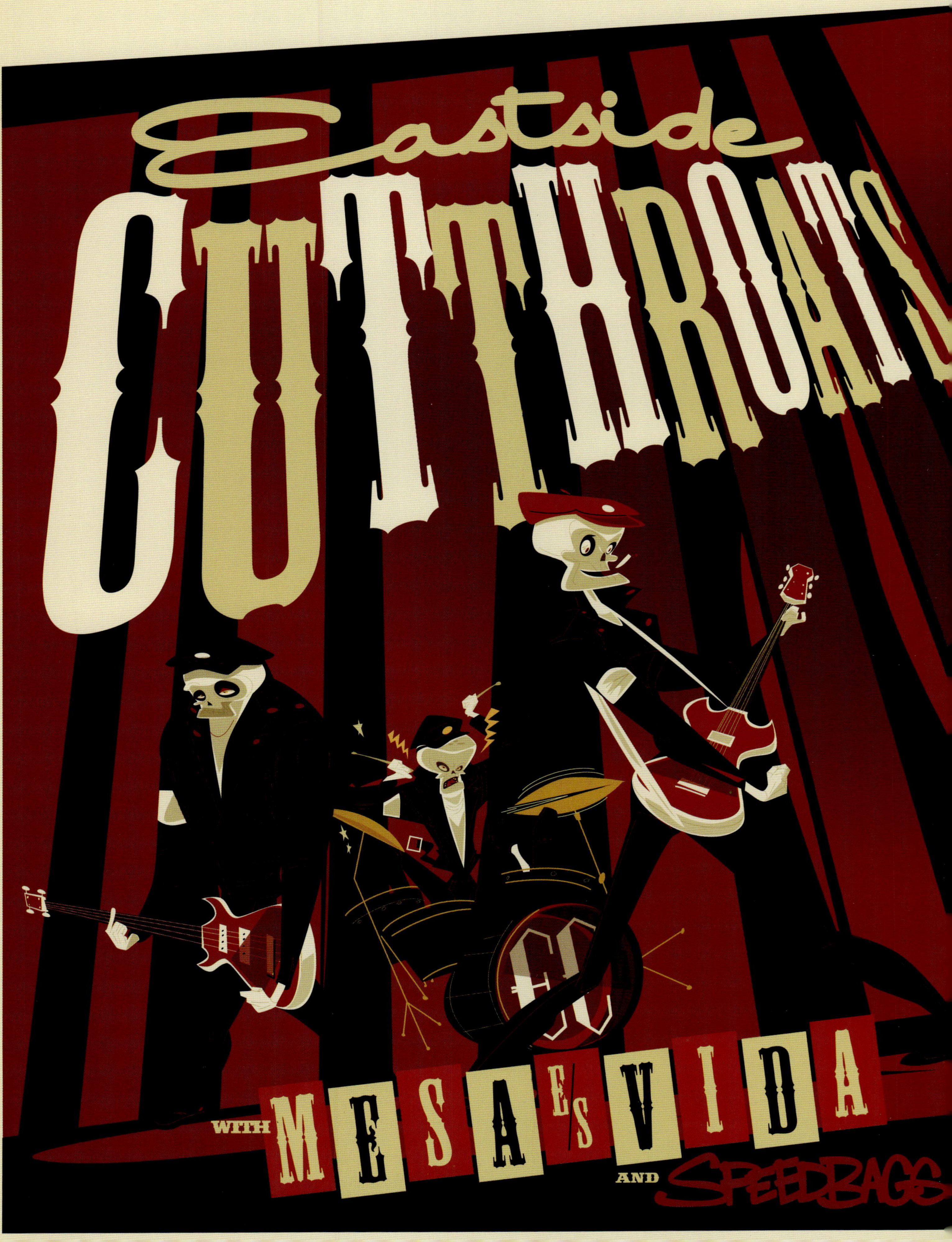

Eastside
CUTTHROATS
WITH MESA/VIDA
AND SPEEDBAGS

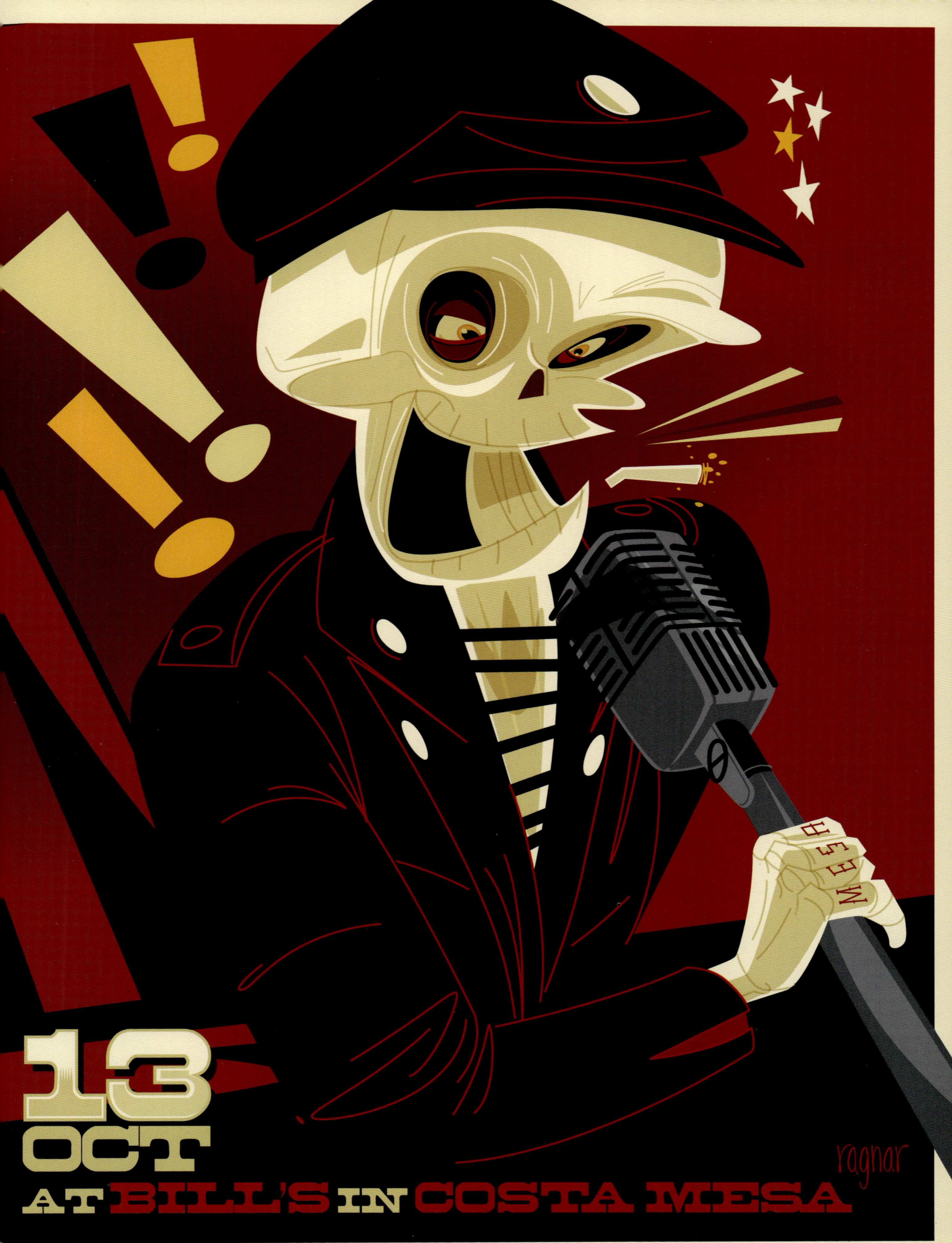
13
OCT
AT BILL'S IN COSTA MESA
ragnar
MESH

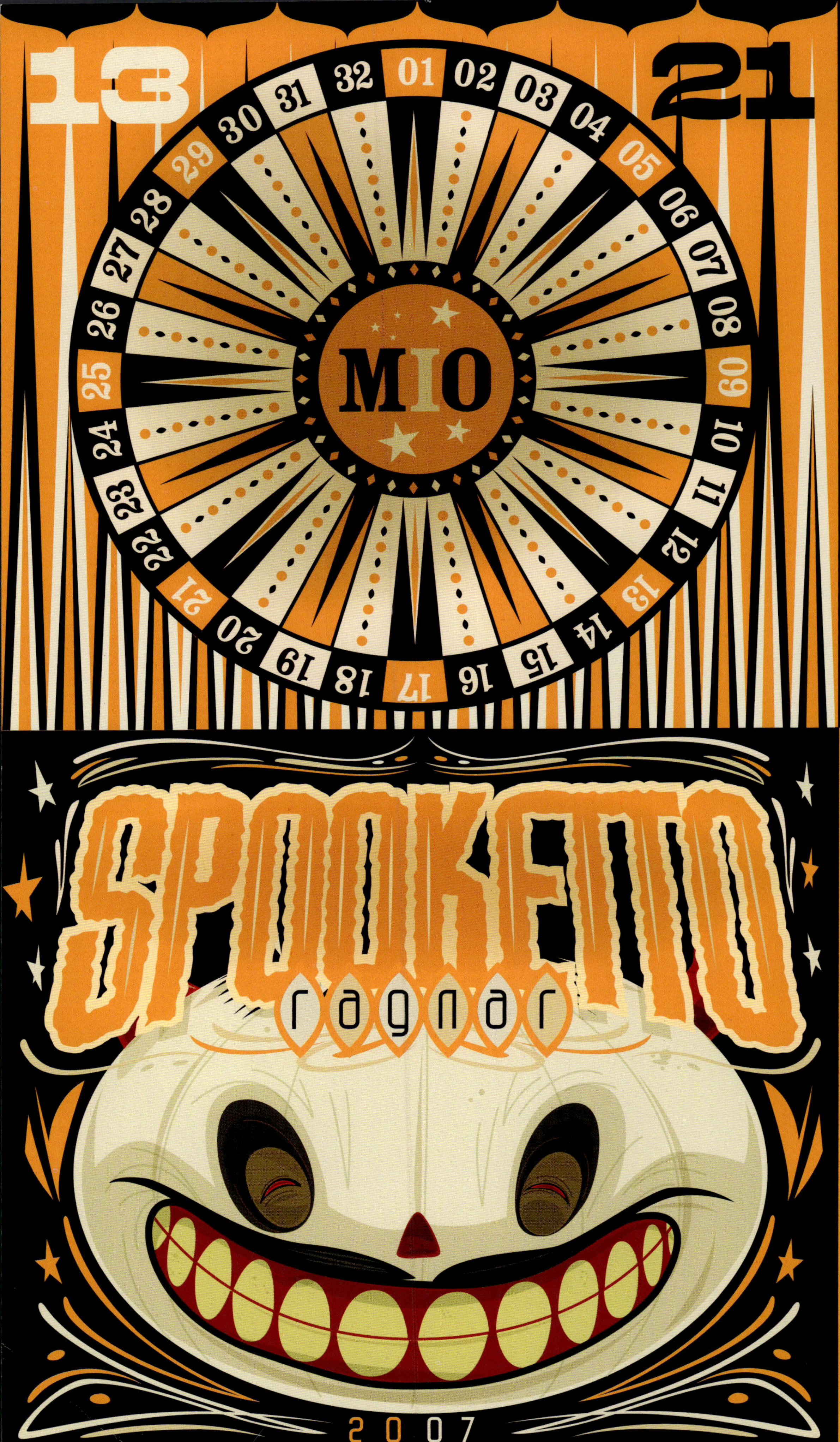

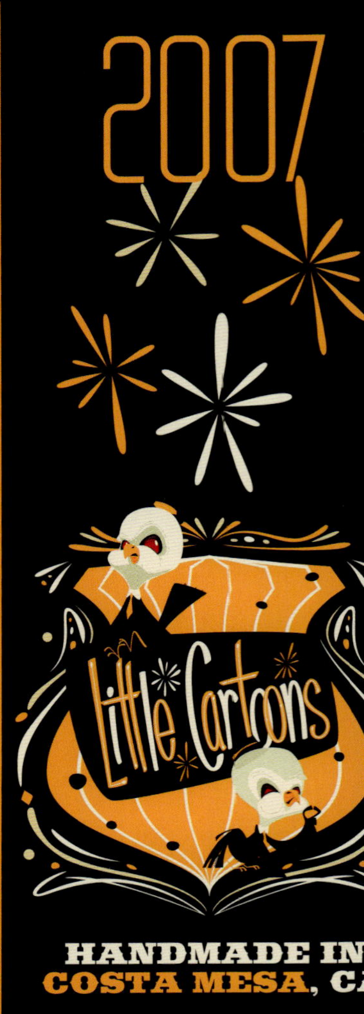

13 21

32 01 02 03 04 05 06 07 08 09 10 11 12 13 14 15 16 17 18 19 20 21 22 23 24 25 26 27 28 29 30 31

MIO

2007

Little Cartoons

**HANDMADE IN
COSTA MESA, CA**

SPOOKETTO

ragnar

2007

Spooketto is a chimera. Born of the union between vintage papier-maché Halloween decorations and that sad clown Pagliacci. While he's been showing up for years in various forms this particular design was created specifically for the inaugural Baby Tattooville event in 2007. I used these designs to sculpt and cast a series of resin Halloween decorations. I tried to maintain the softly defined edges and contours of the papier-mâché decorations which inspred it. The birds have been loafing about for years as well.

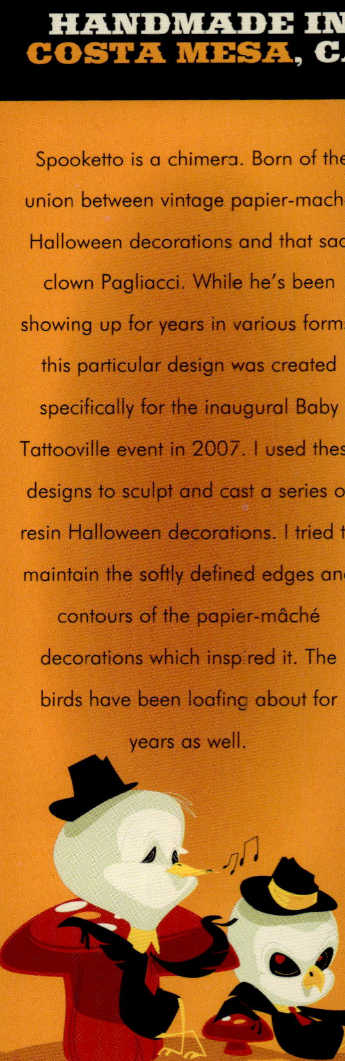

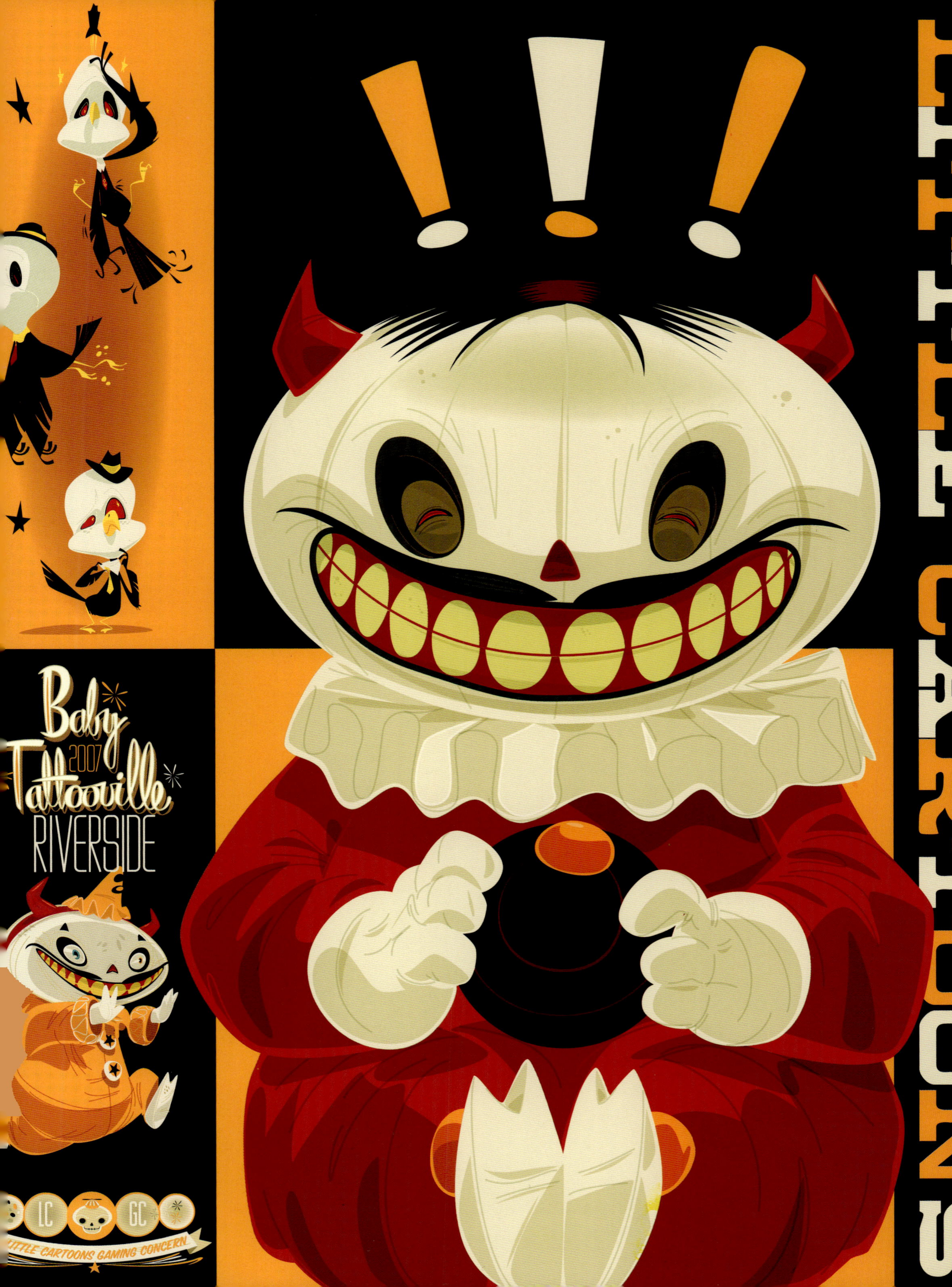

LITTLE CARTOONS
Baby
2007
Tattooville
RIVERSIDE
LC
GC
LITTLE CARTOONS GAMING CONCERN

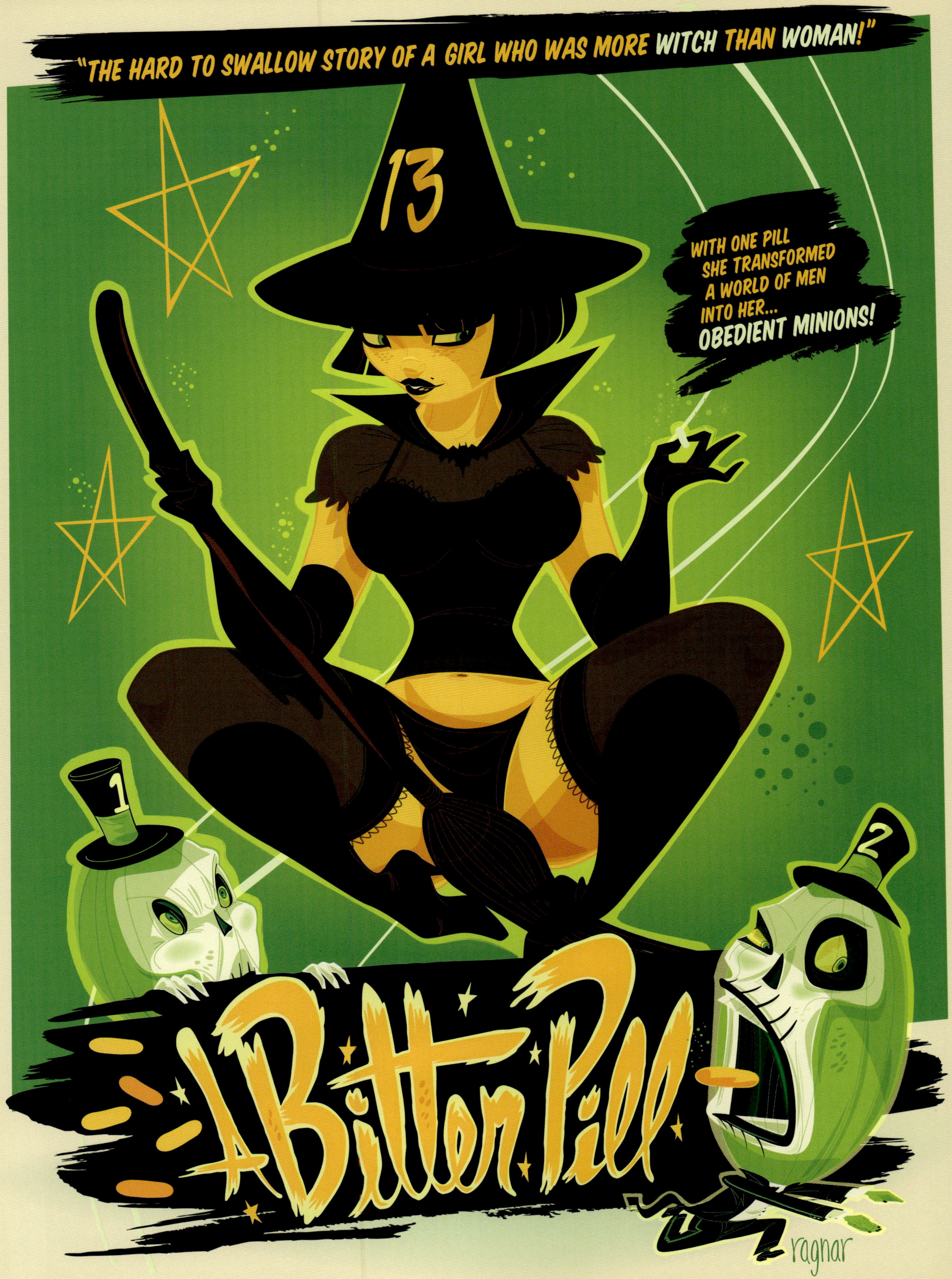

"THE HARD TO SWALLOW STORY OF A GIRL WHO WAS MORE WITCH THAN WOMAN!"
13
WITH ONE PILL SHE TRANSFORMED A WORLD OF MEN INTO HER... OBEDIENT MINIONS!
1
2
A Bitter Pill
ragnar

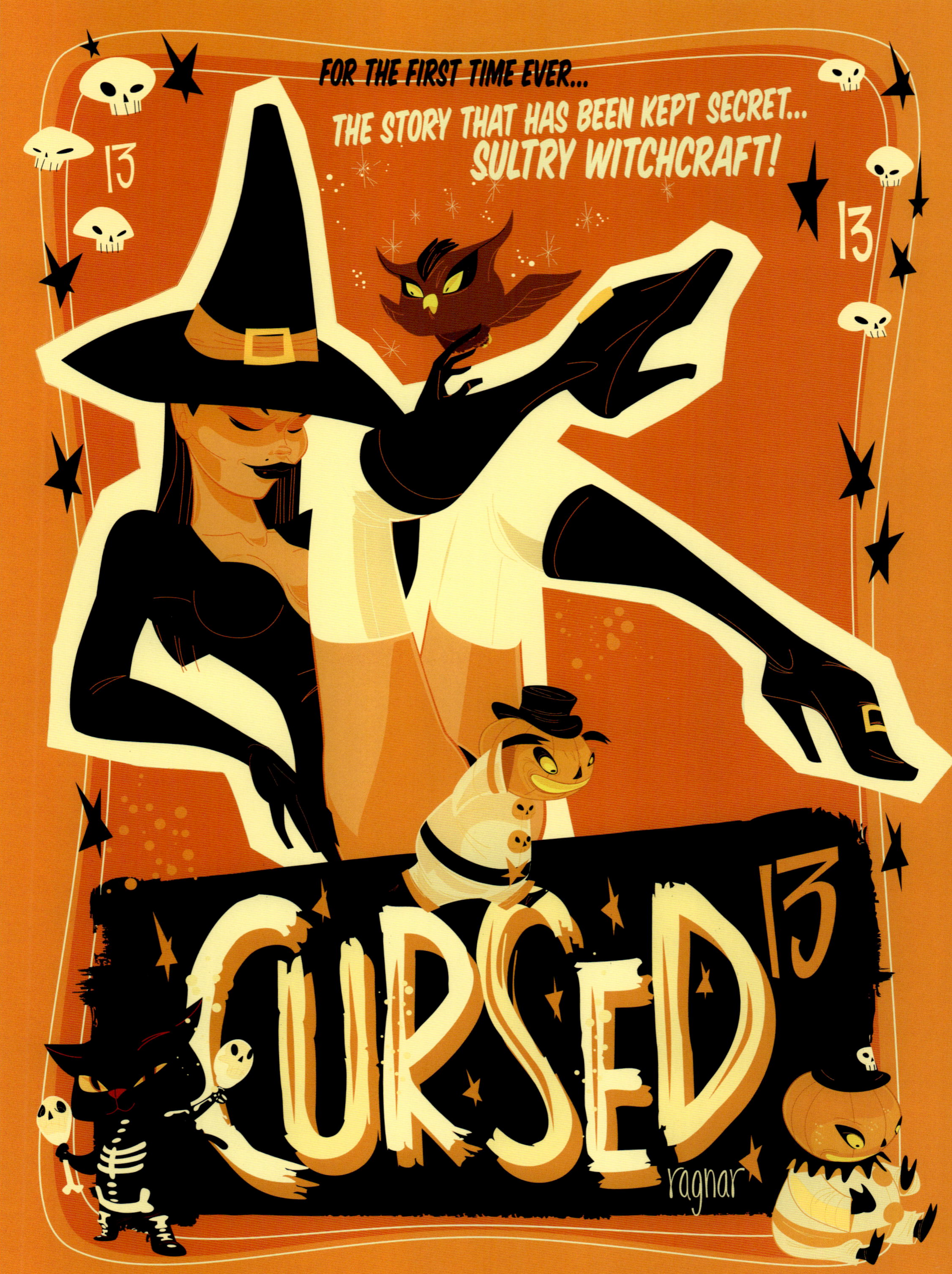
FOR THE FIRST TIME EVER...
THE STORY THAT HAS BEEN KEPT SECRET...
SULTRY WITCHCRAFT!
13
13
CURSED 13
ragnar

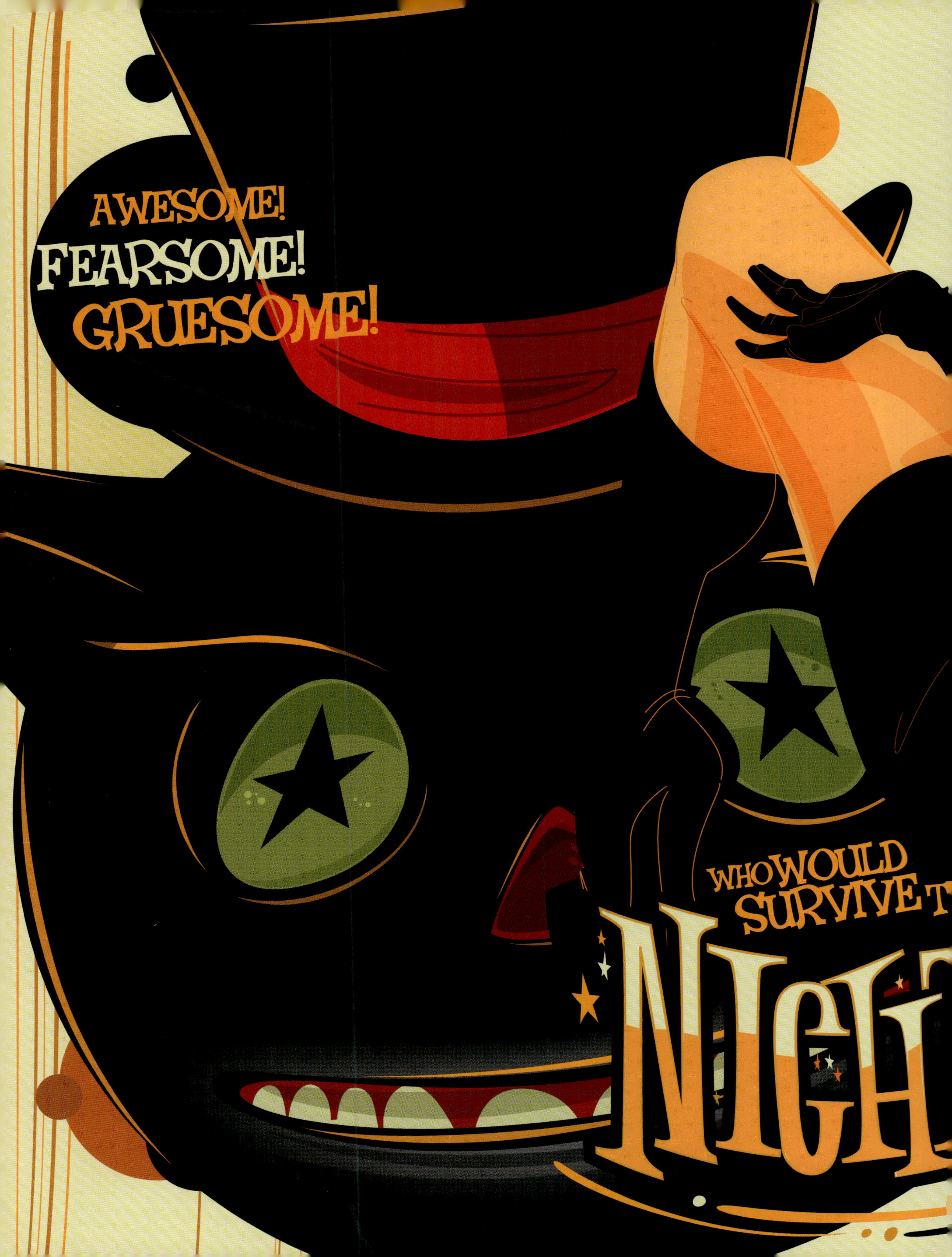
AWESOME!
FEARSOME!
GRUESOME!
WHO WOULD SURVIVE T
NIGH

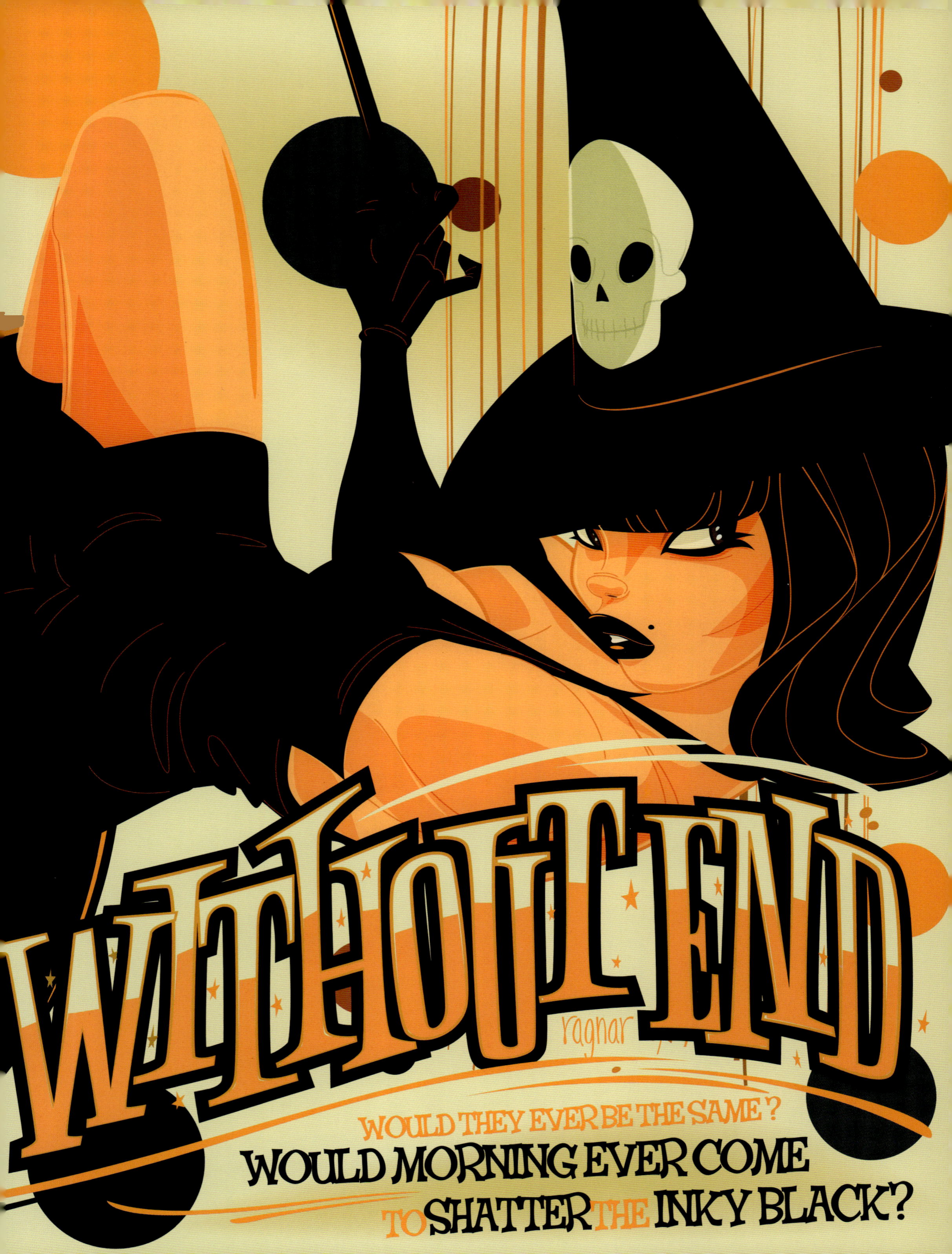

WITHOUT END
ragnar
WOULD THEY EVER BE THE SAME?
WOULD MORNING EVER COME
TO SHATTER THE INKY BLACK?

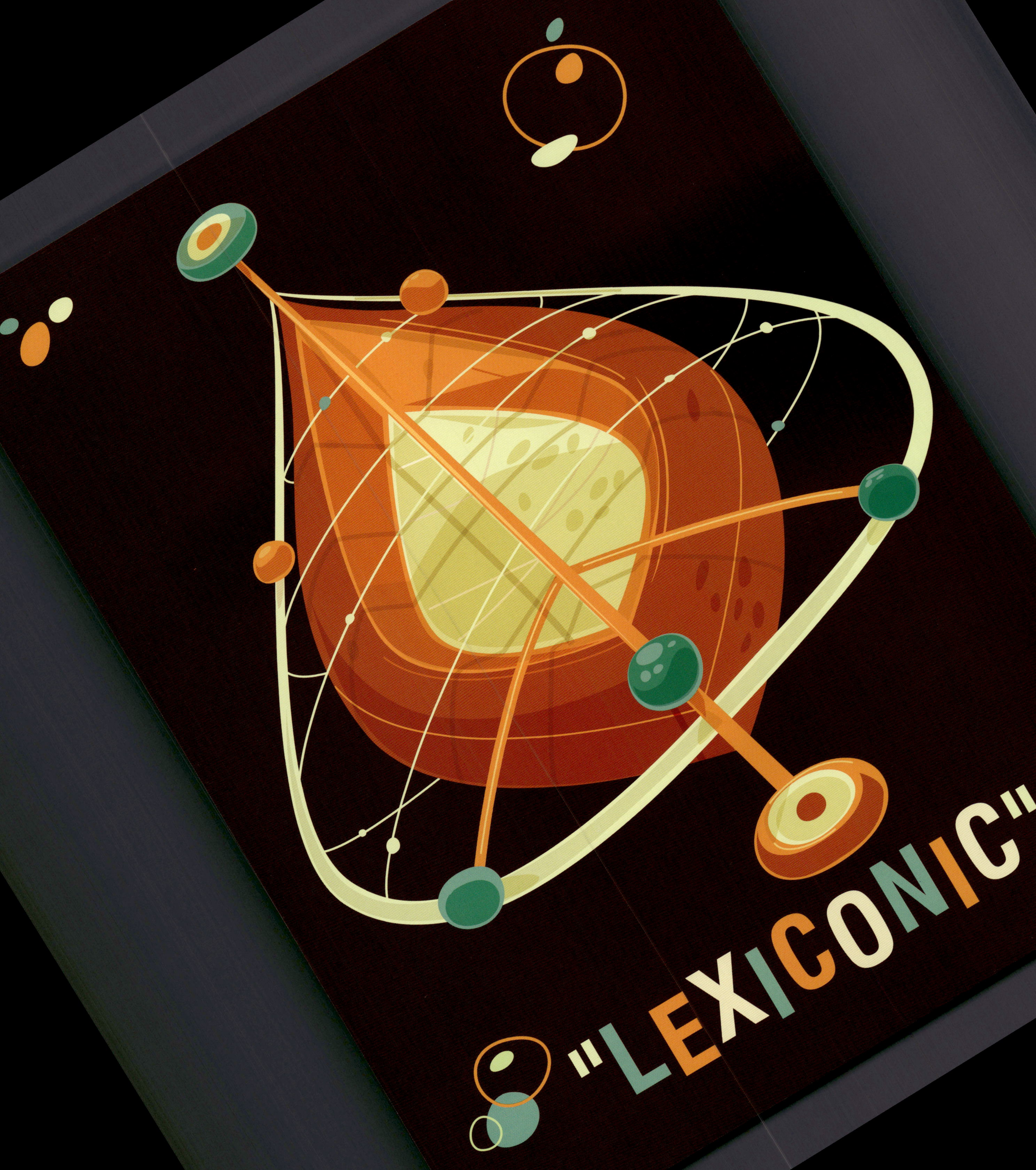
"LEXICONIC"

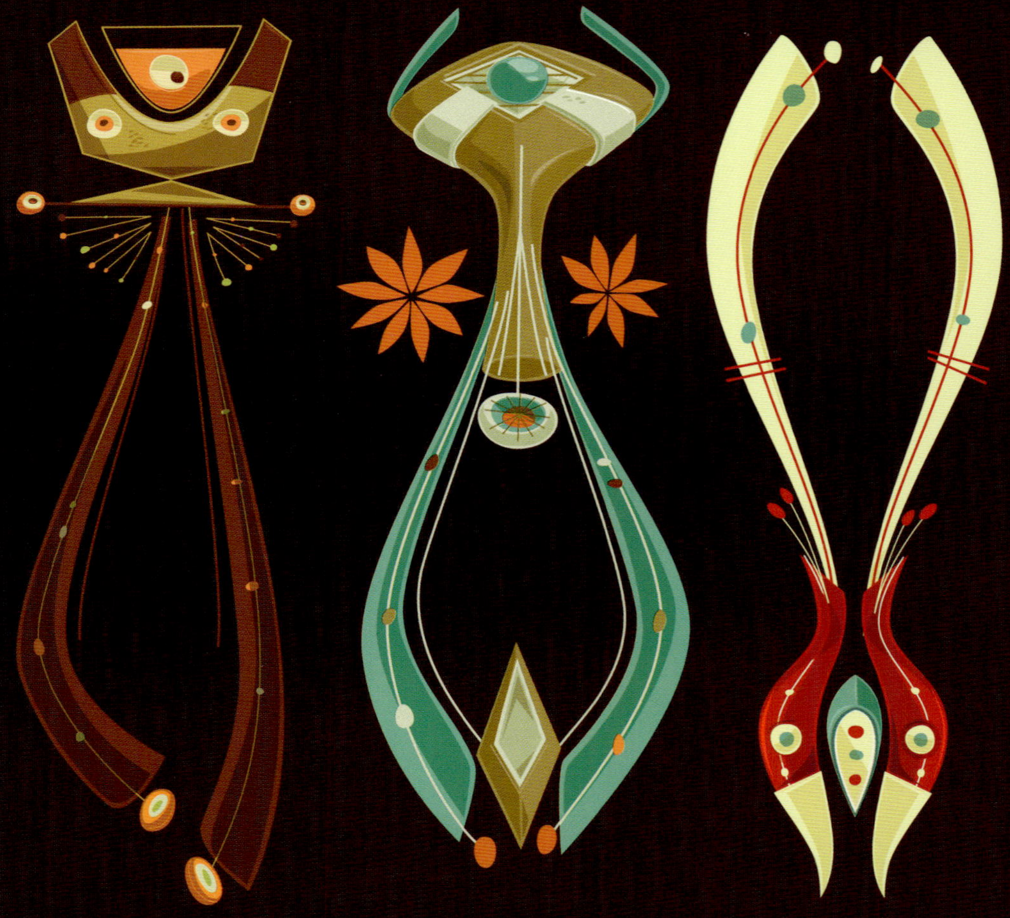

I don't care for irony. It's a thin, flimsy approach. Phony reverence without any real investment or commitment. It's the bastard child of kitsch bereft of whimsy and humor.

This is chronologically the most recent work in this book and best illustrates the transition I've made to come full circle to traditional materials and techniques. The darker, slightly less analogous pallet, the dense layered compositions provided a respite from the distilled and rigid work of the previous few years. The forms are a bit more organic and robust and more illustration than shorthanded design.

I wanted to move the decorative elements that have occupied the backgrounds of my work for years front and center. There's a bounty of riches back there. Those dingbats, curlycues and widgets have become sentient. If the Windows girls are erudite and sophisticated, the Lexiconic girls are base, vulgar and profane (qualities as real–probably more real–than the "good" girls').

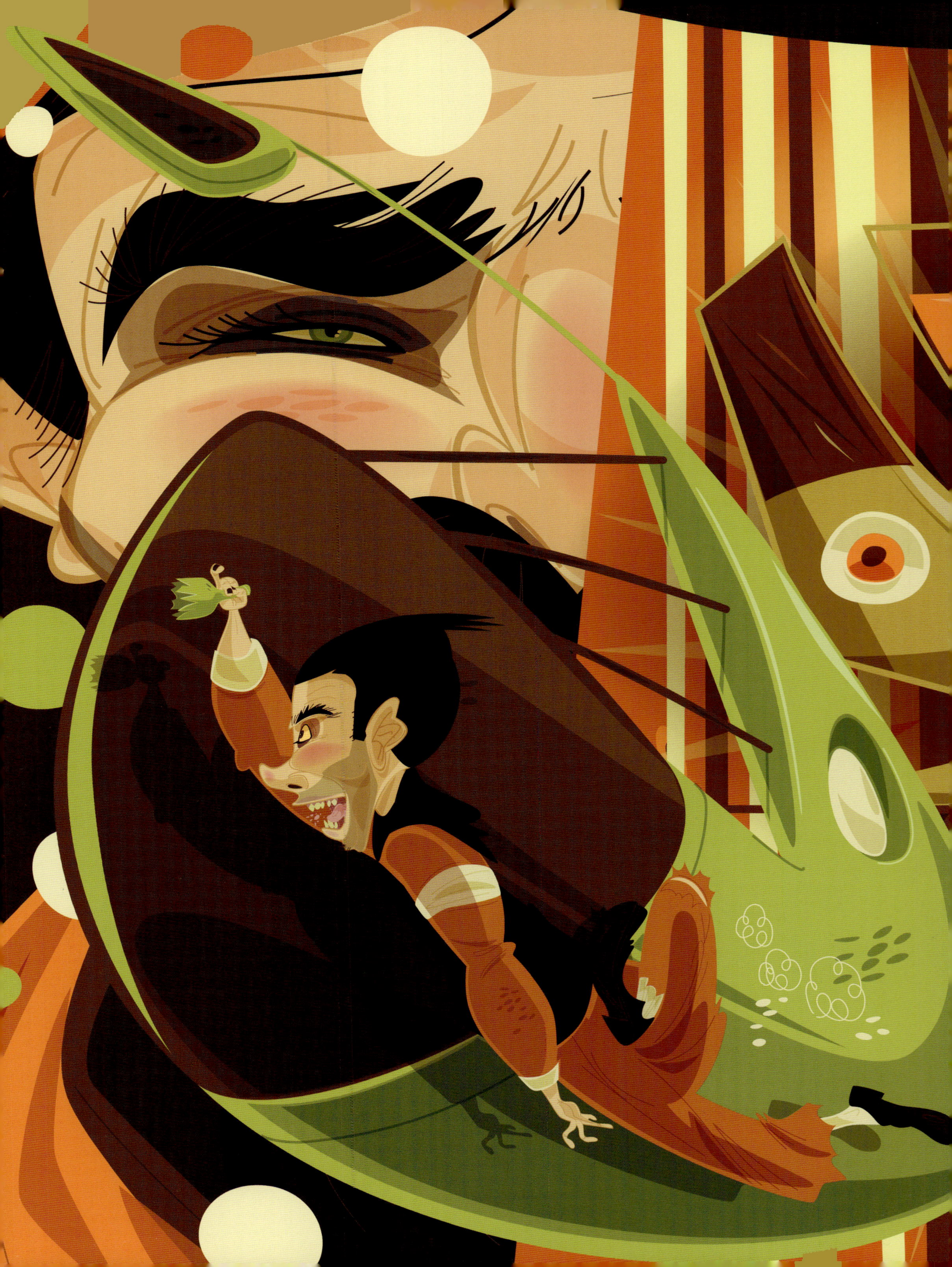

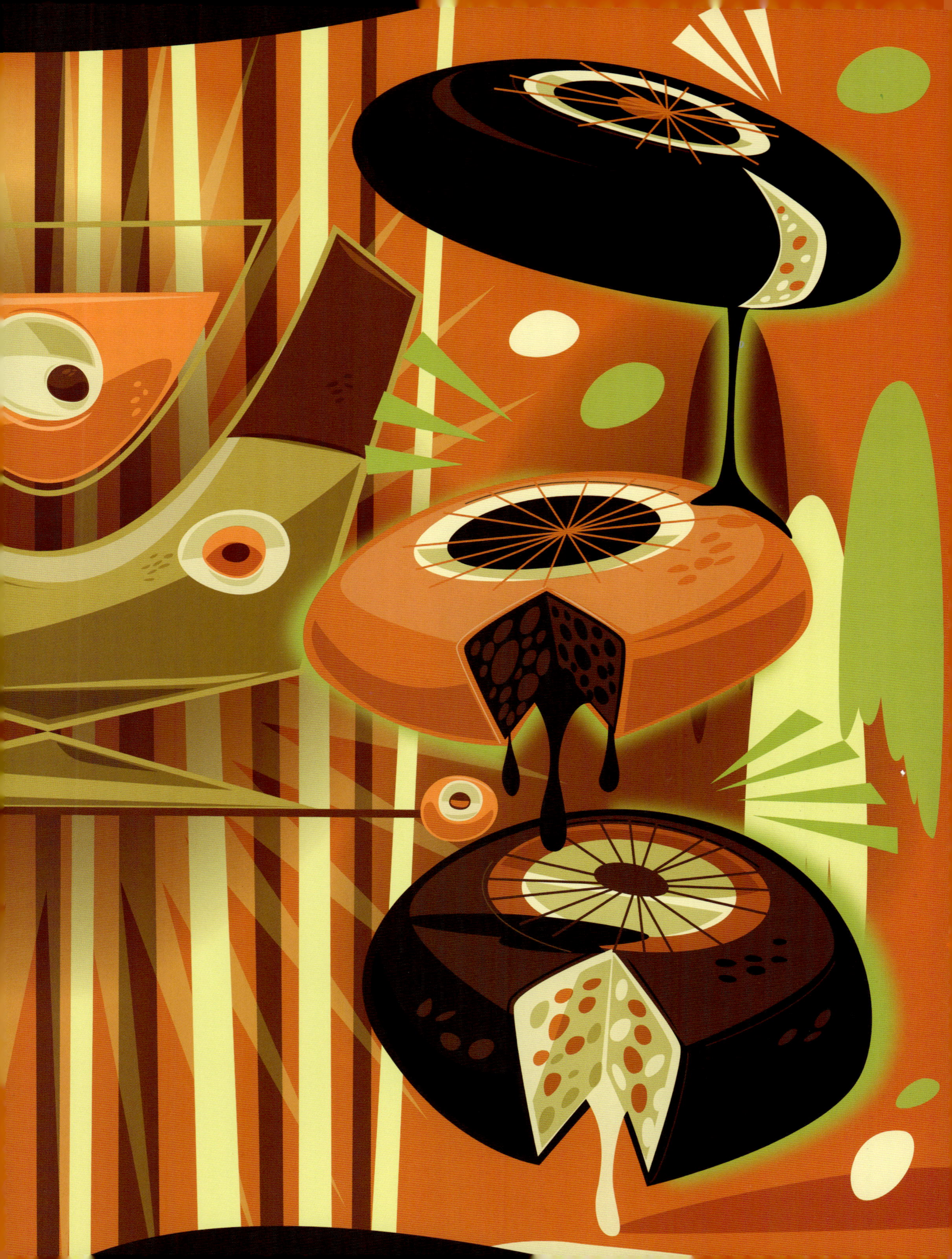

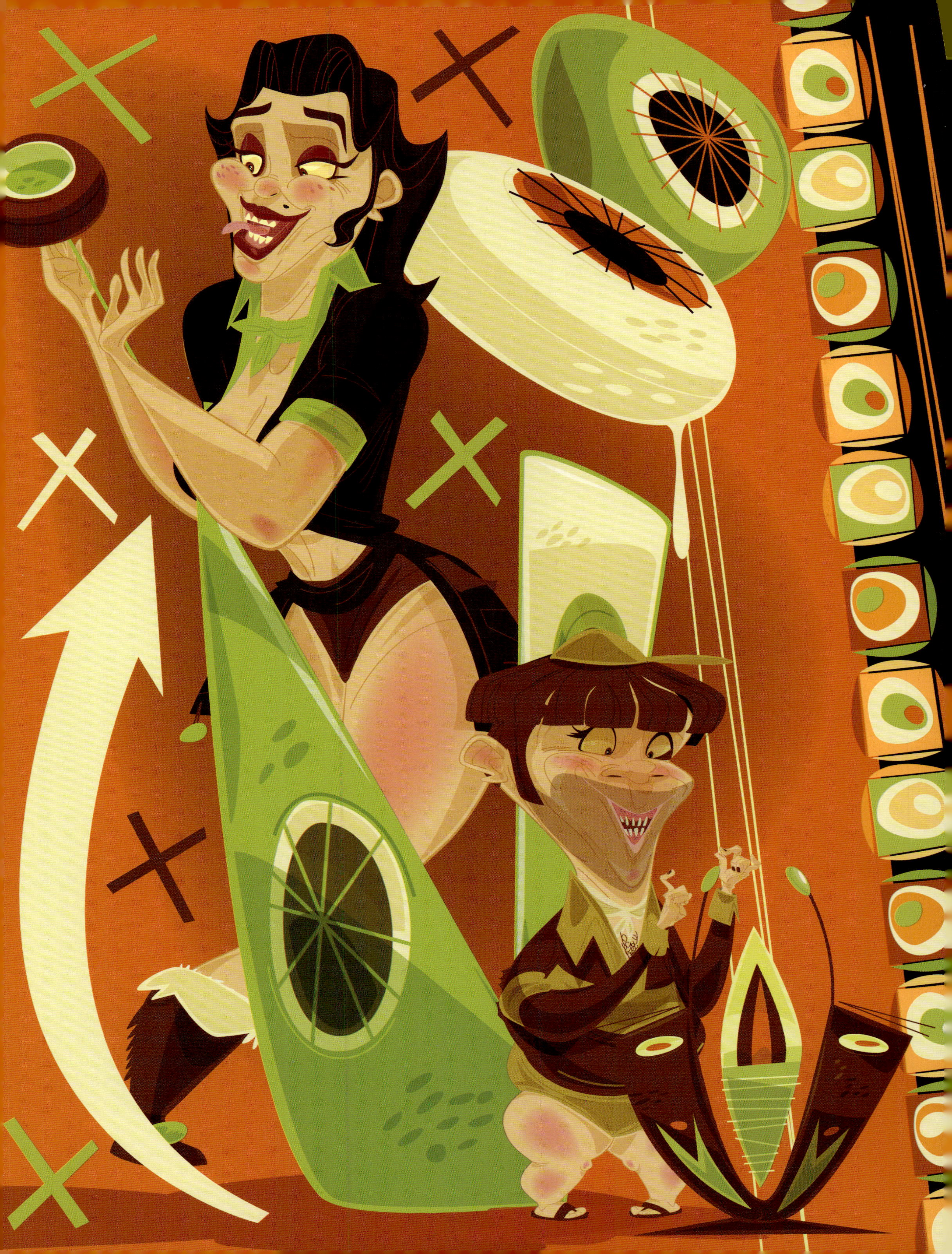

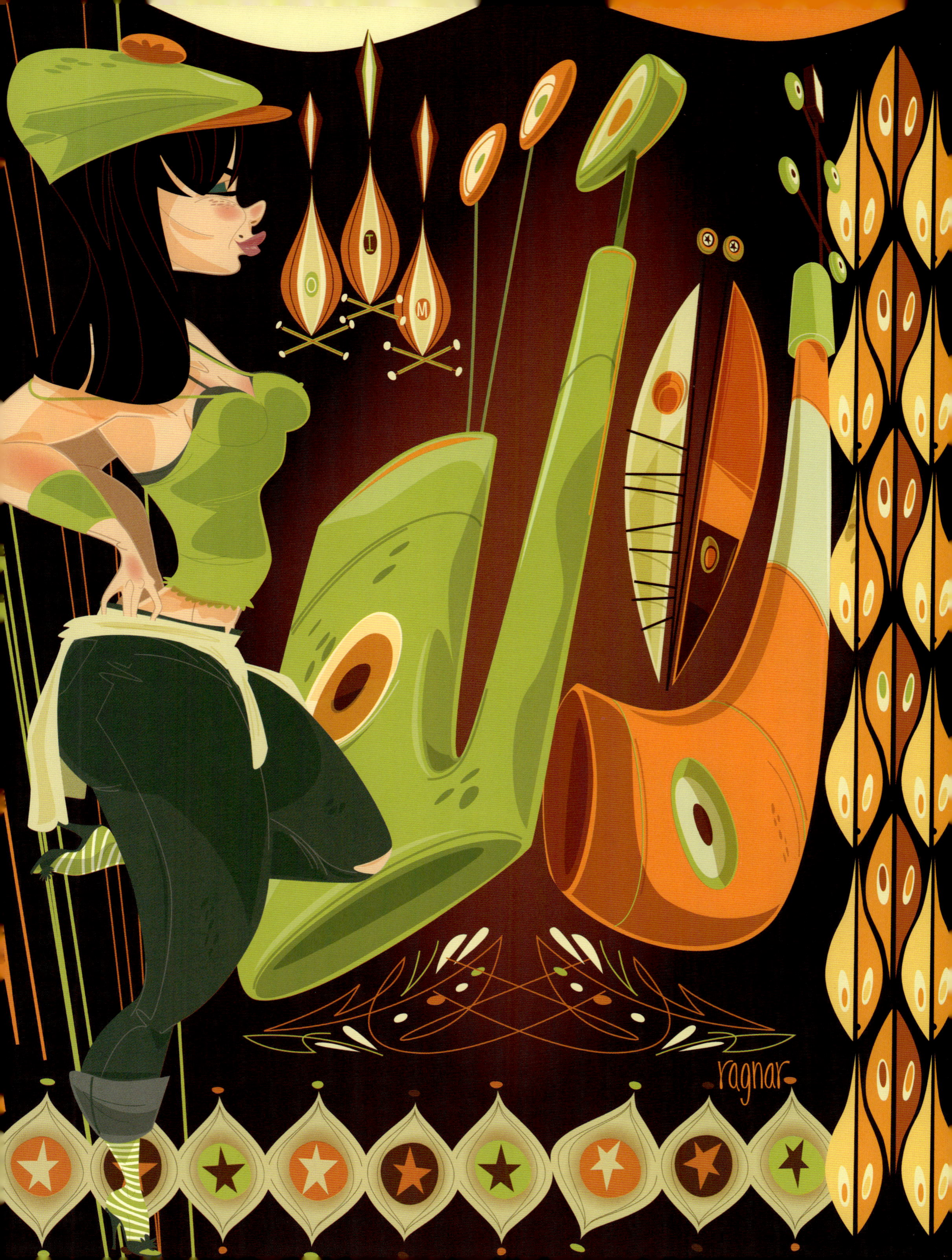

O
I
M
ragnar

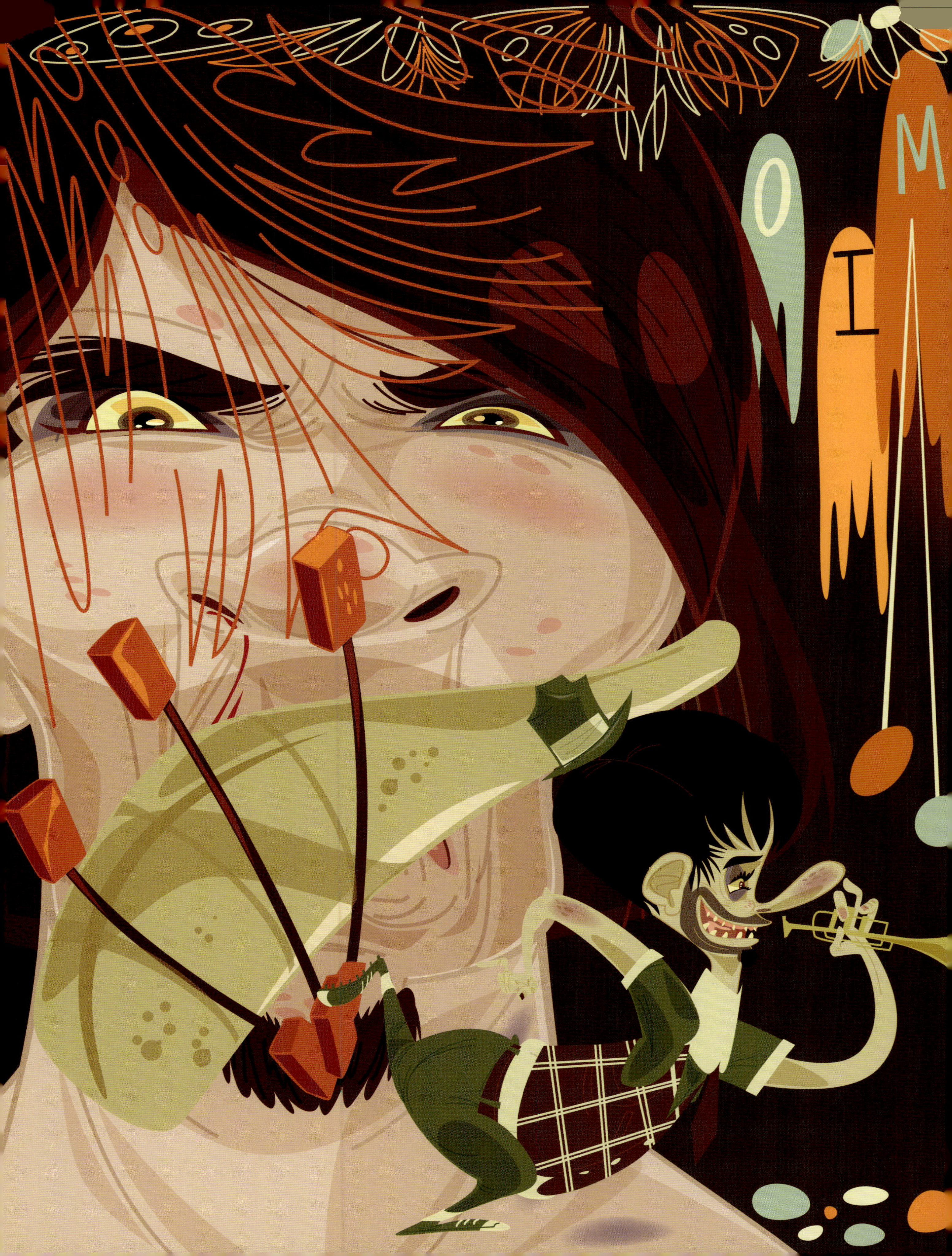
O
M
I

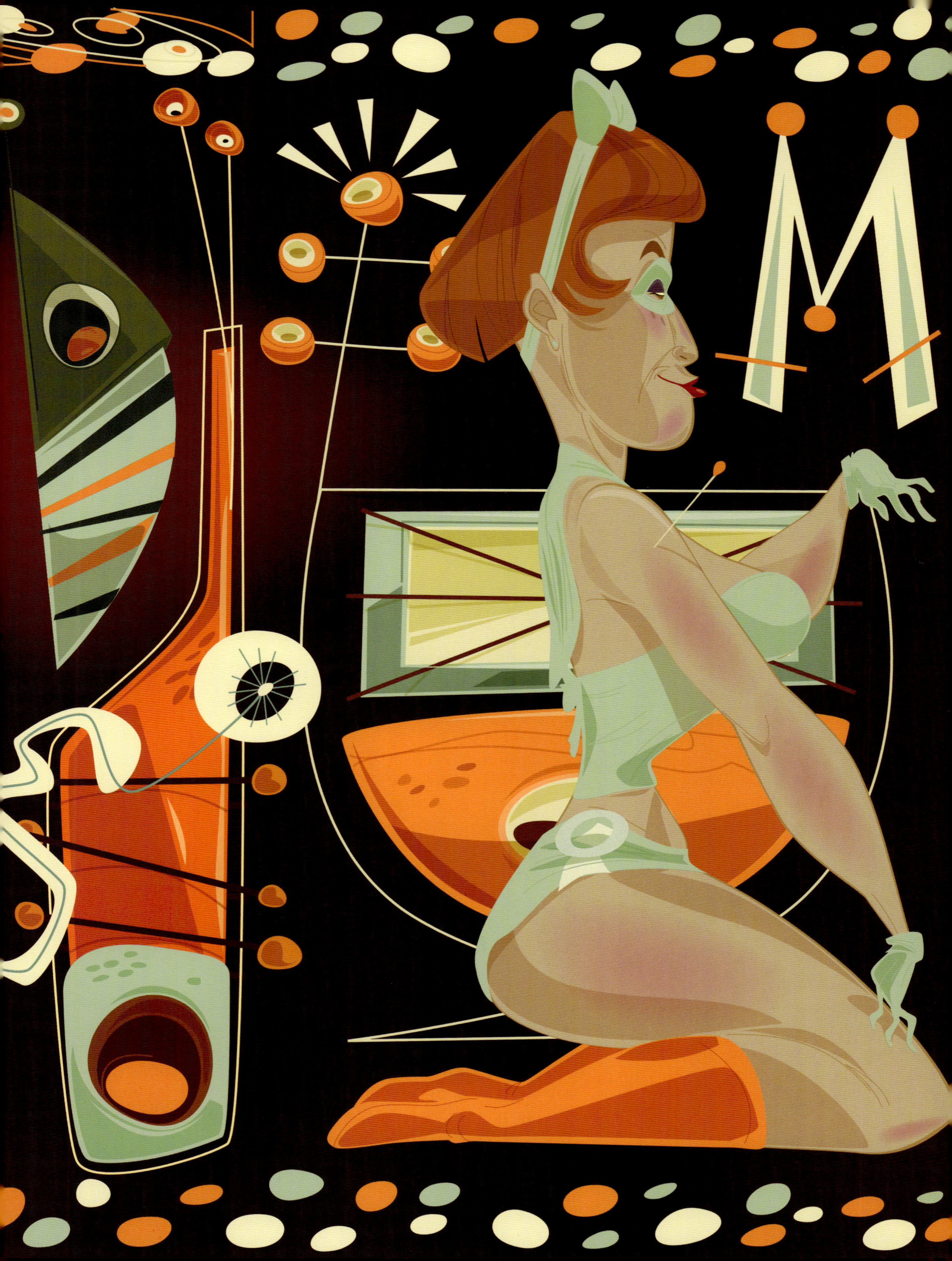

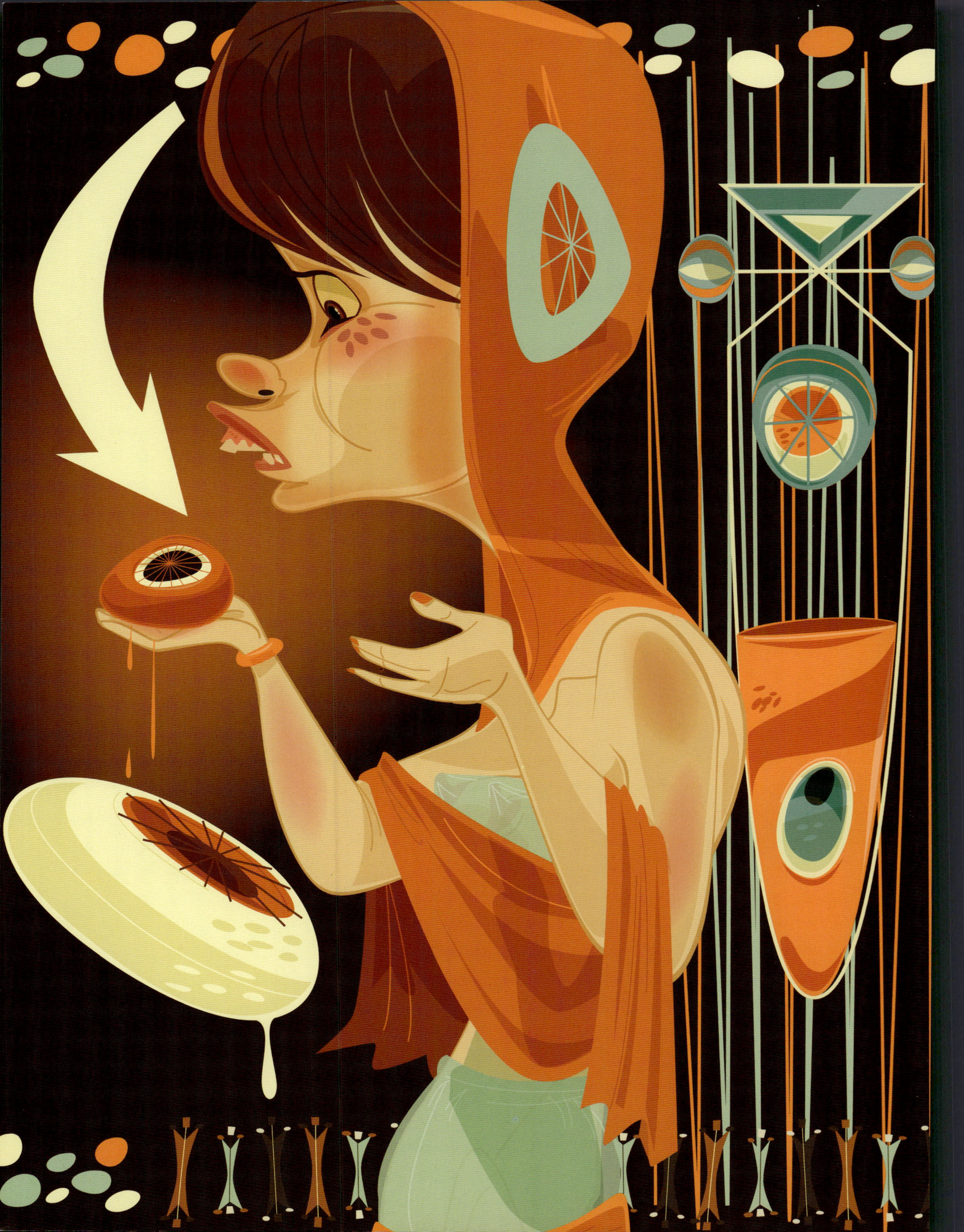

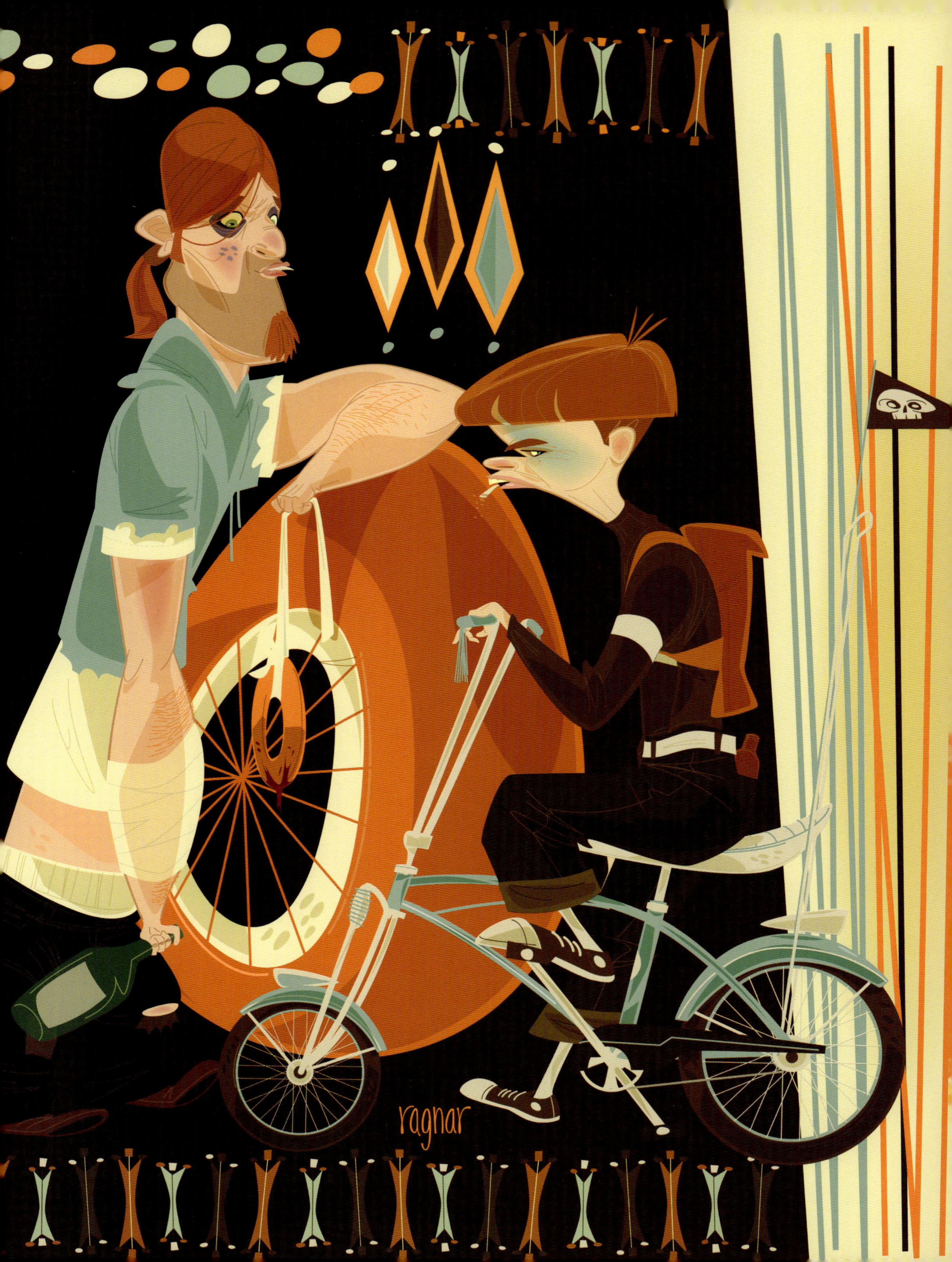

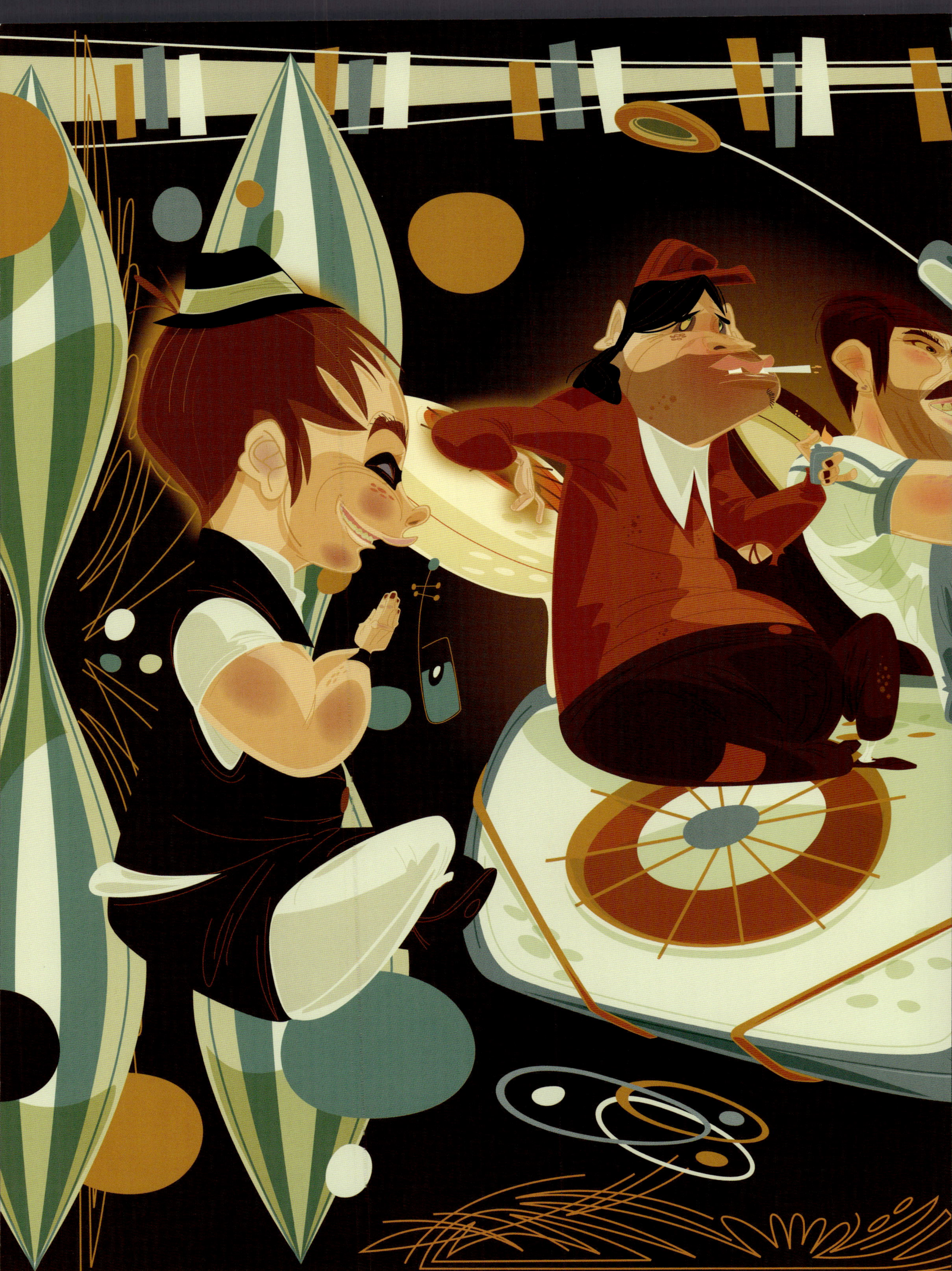

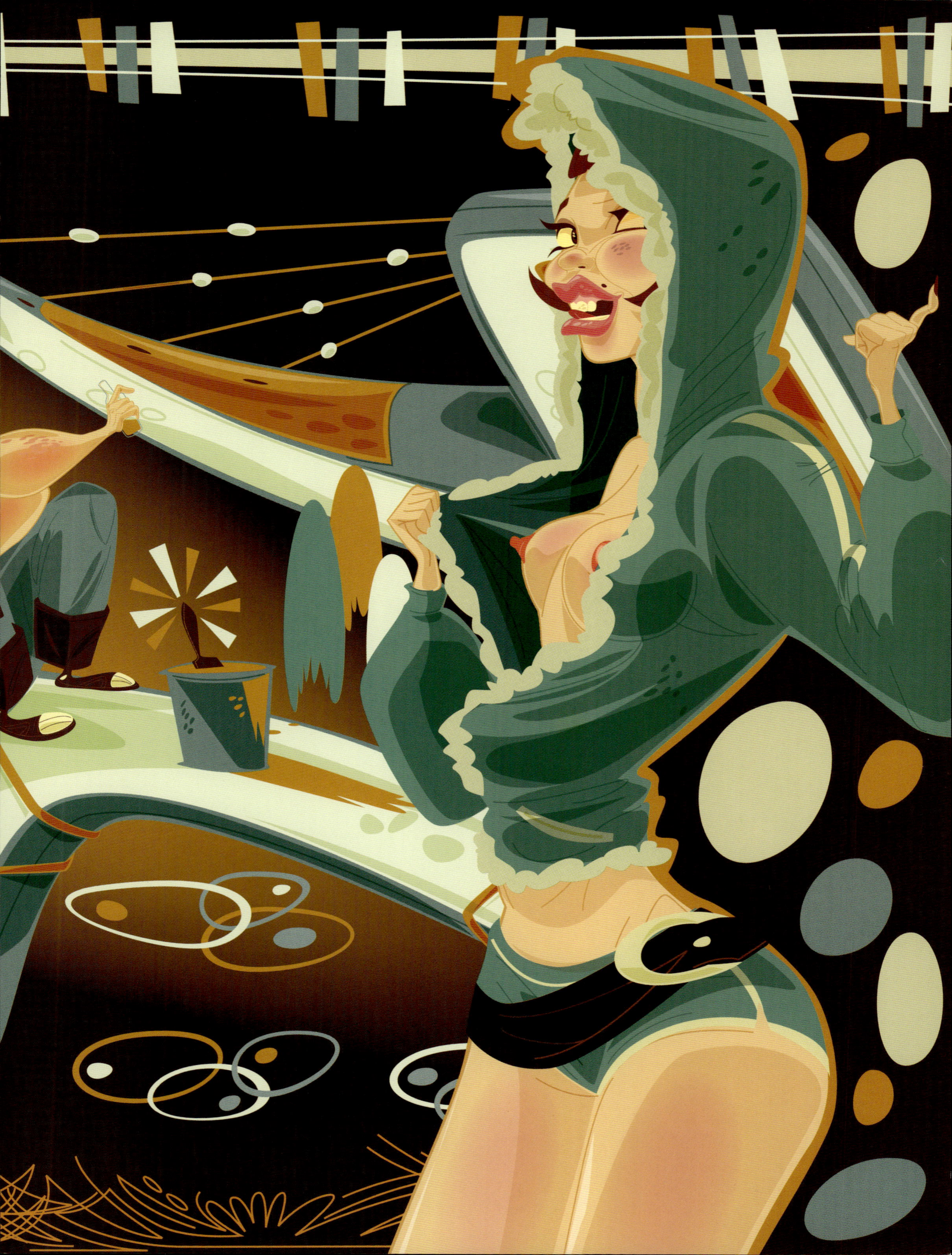

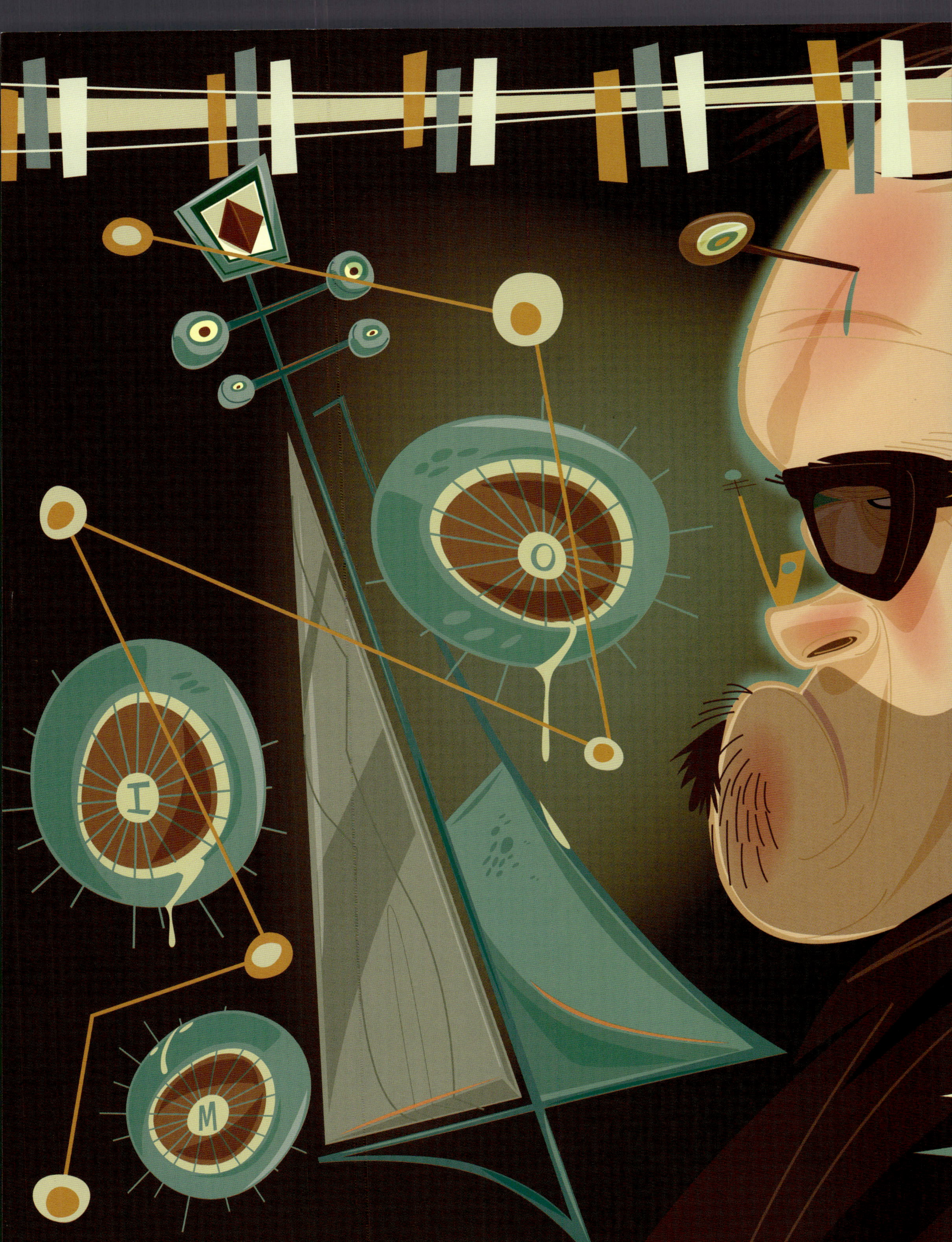

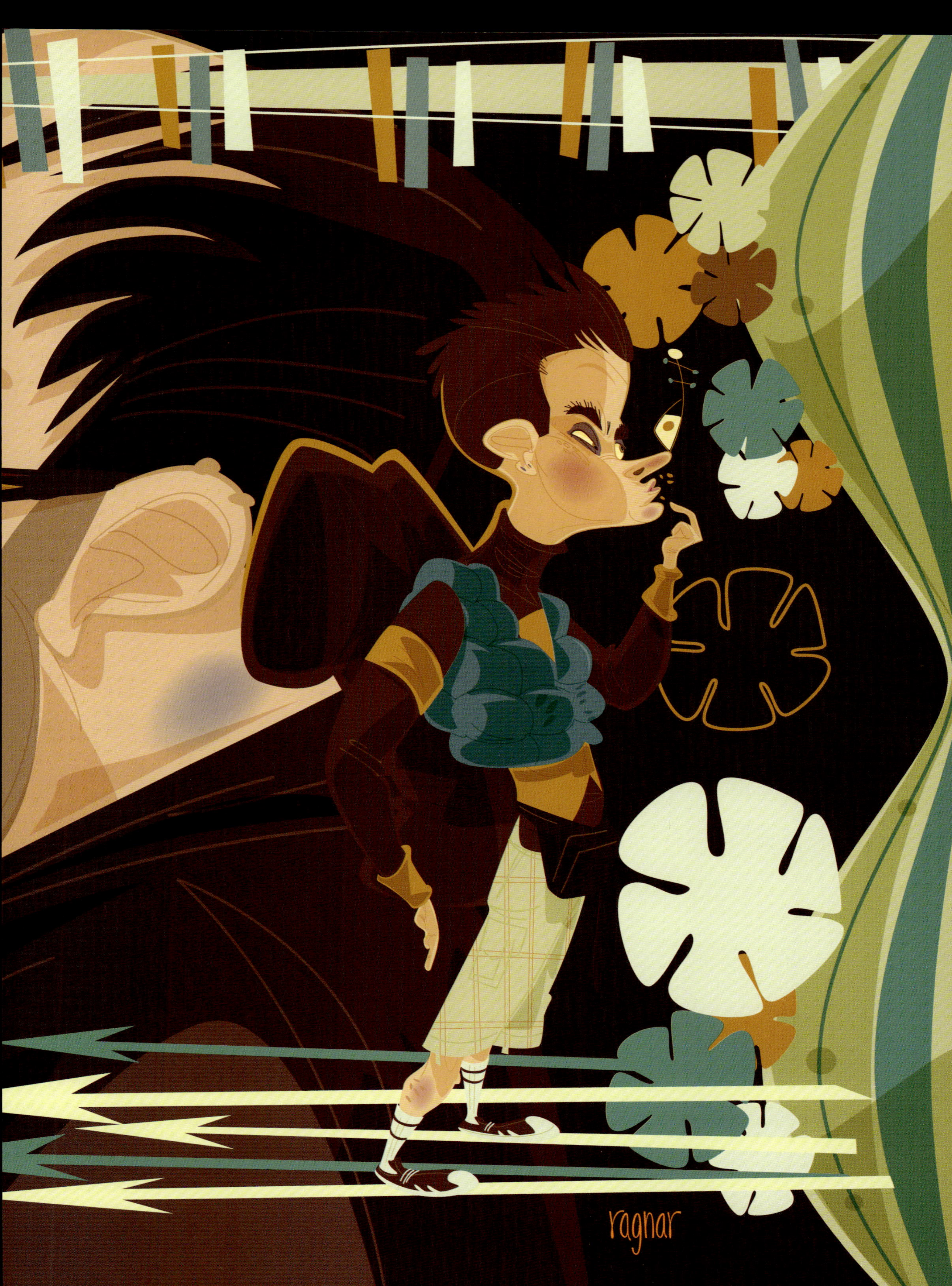
ragnar

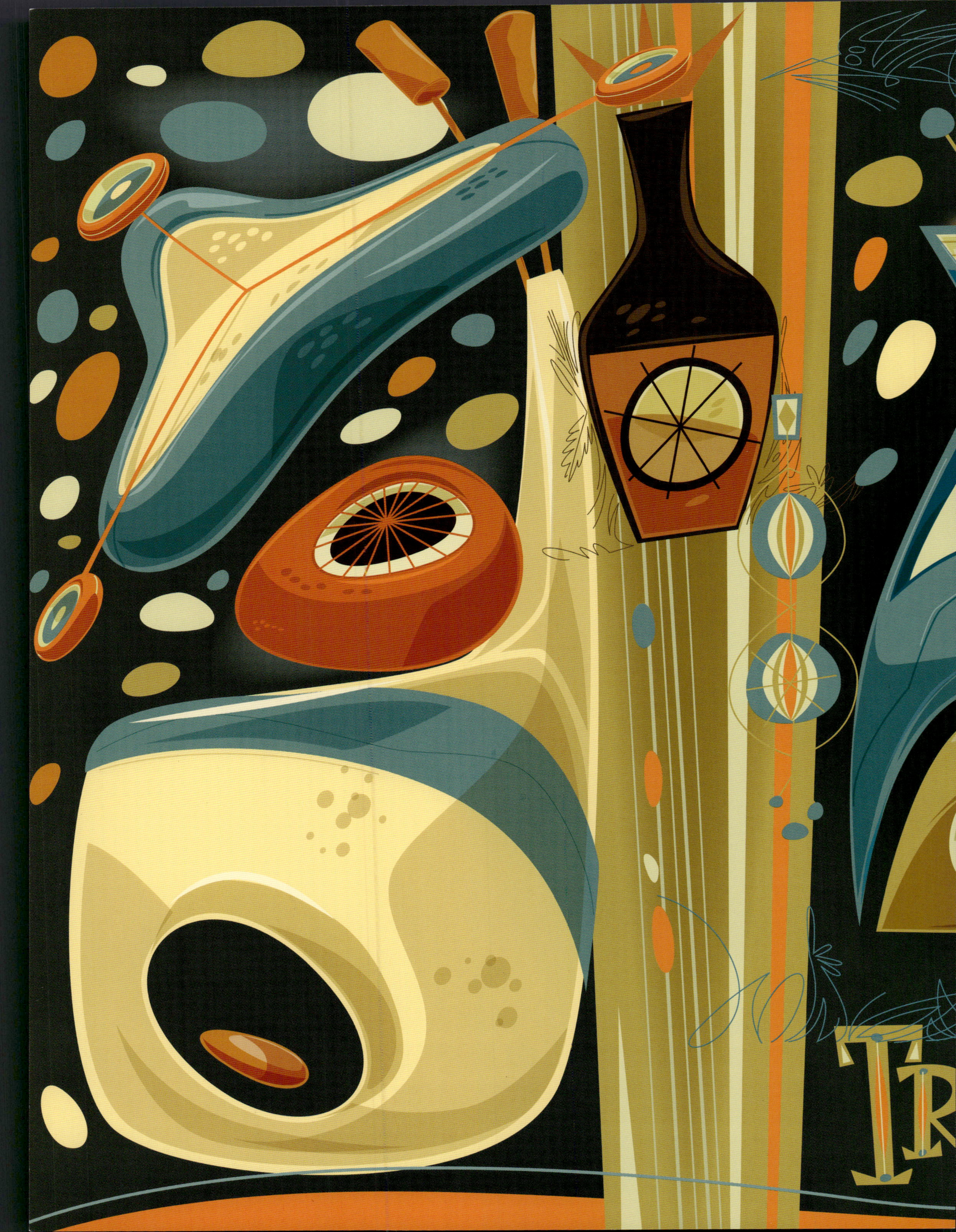

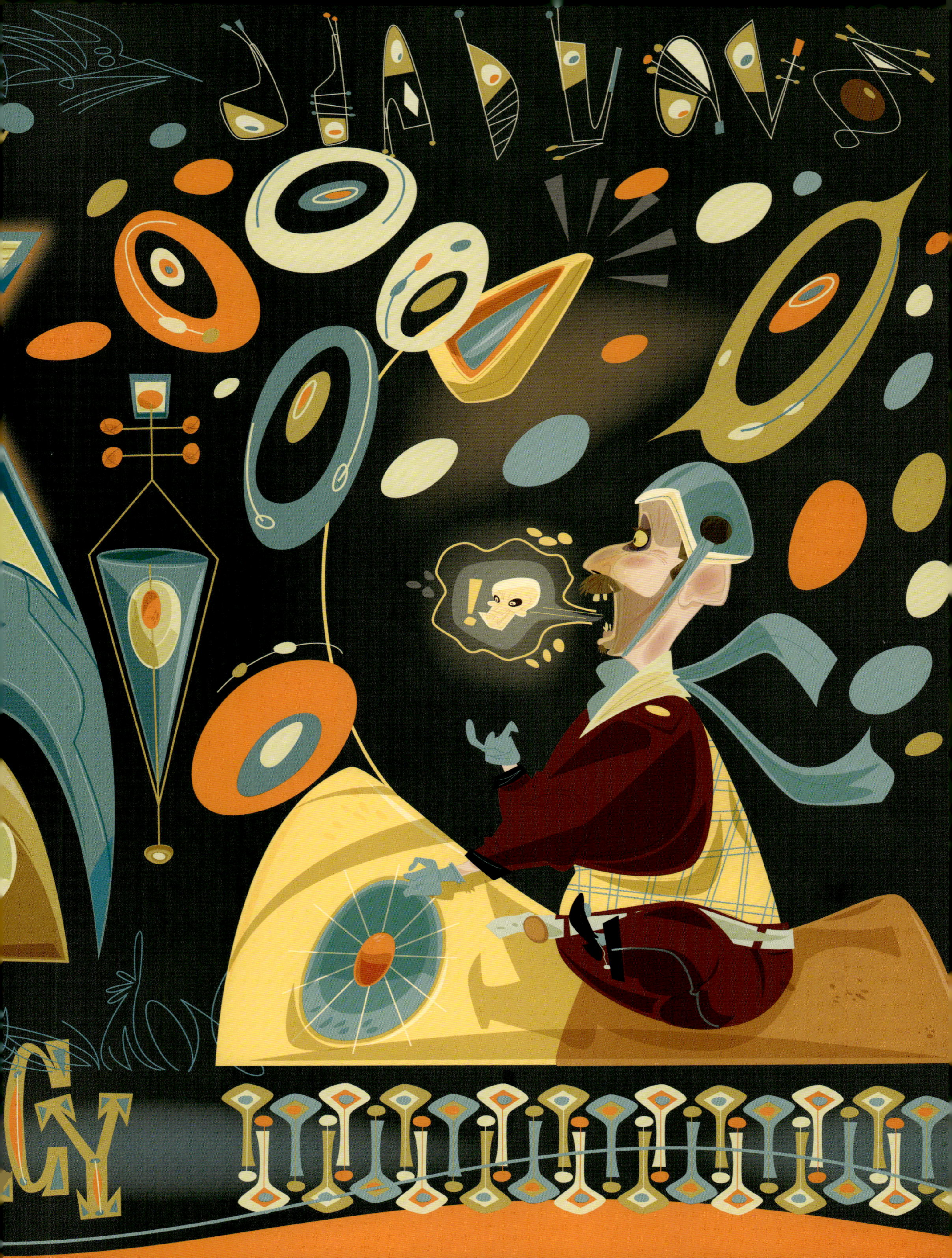

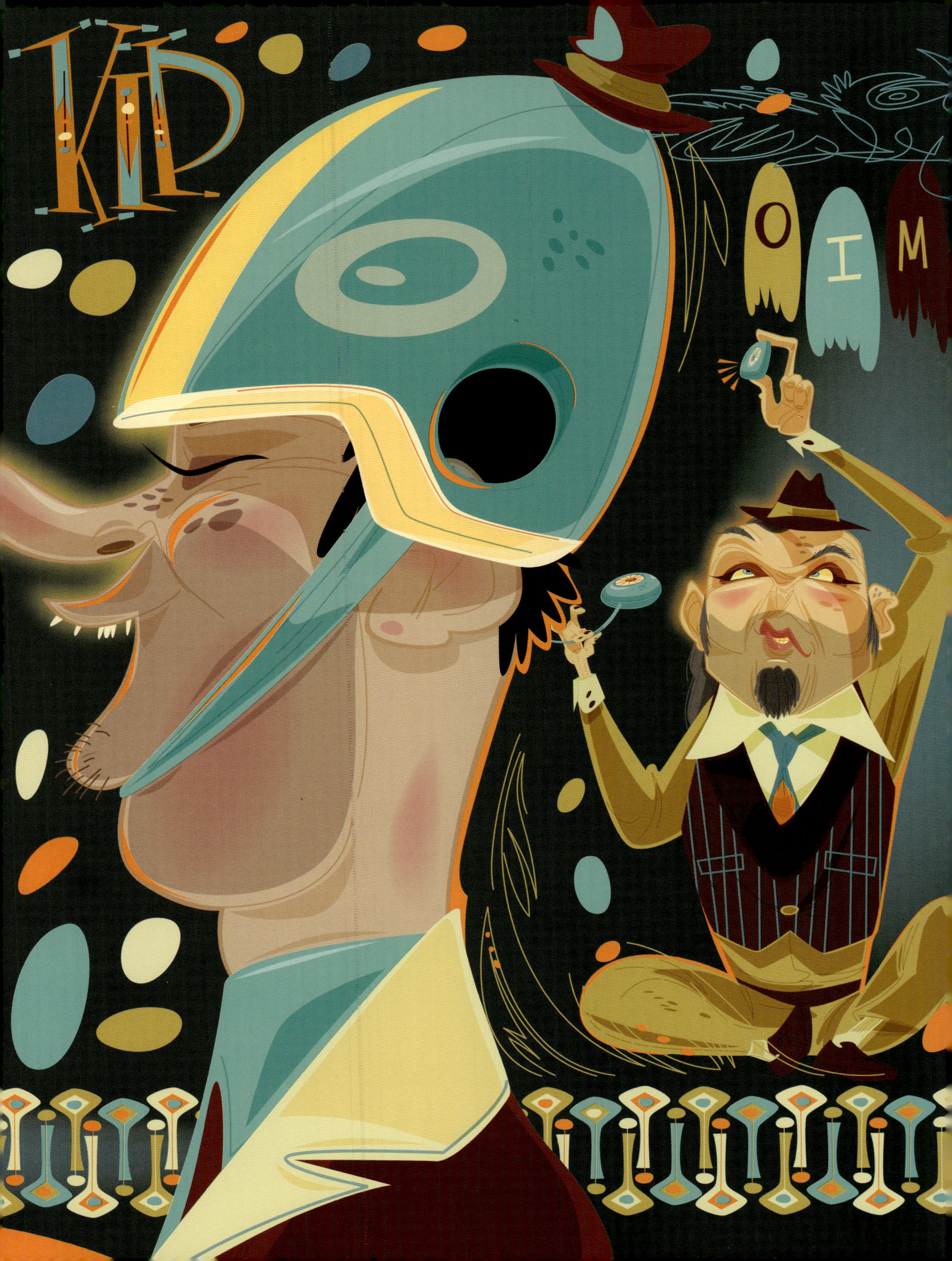
KID
OIM

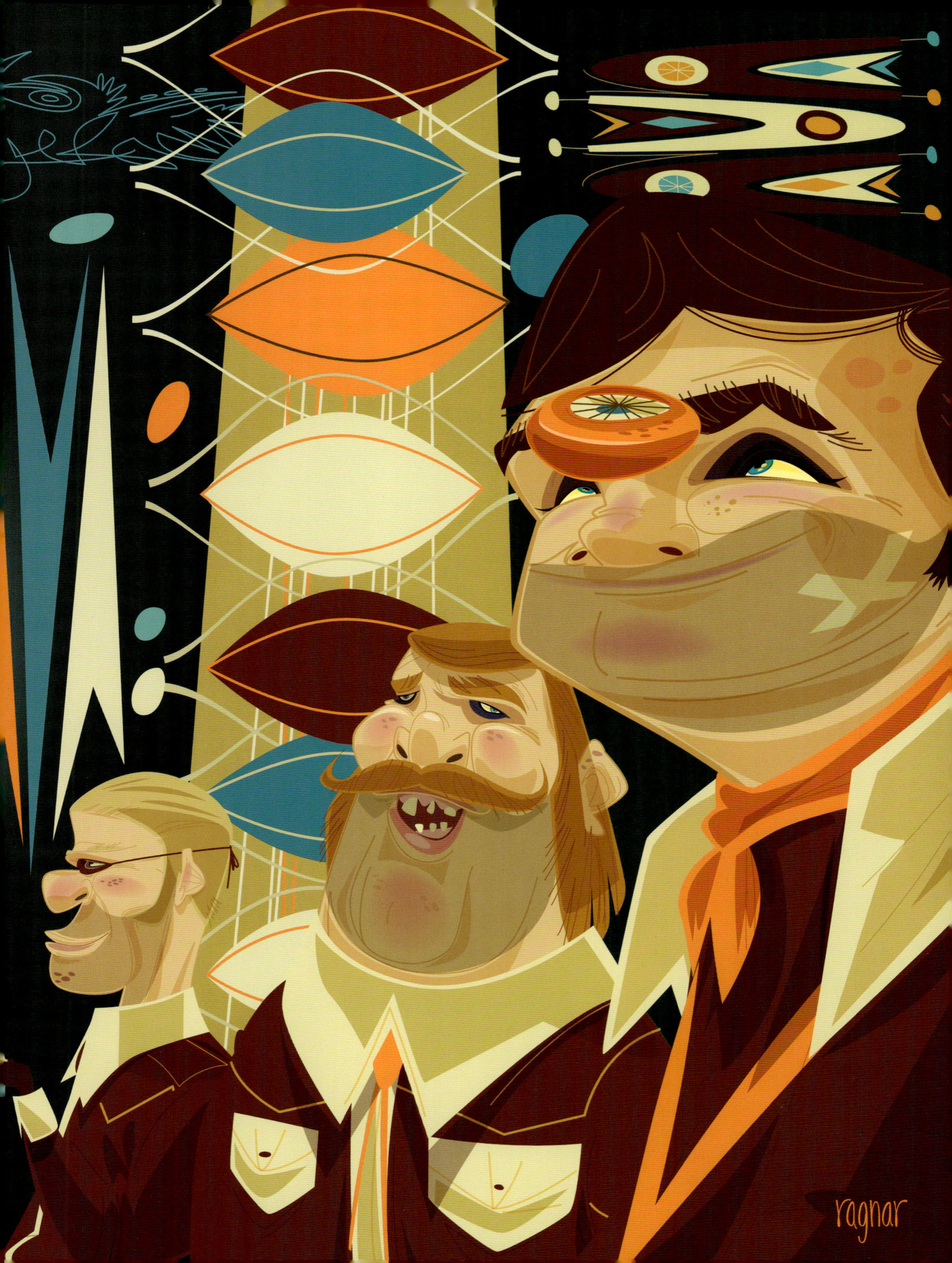
ragnar

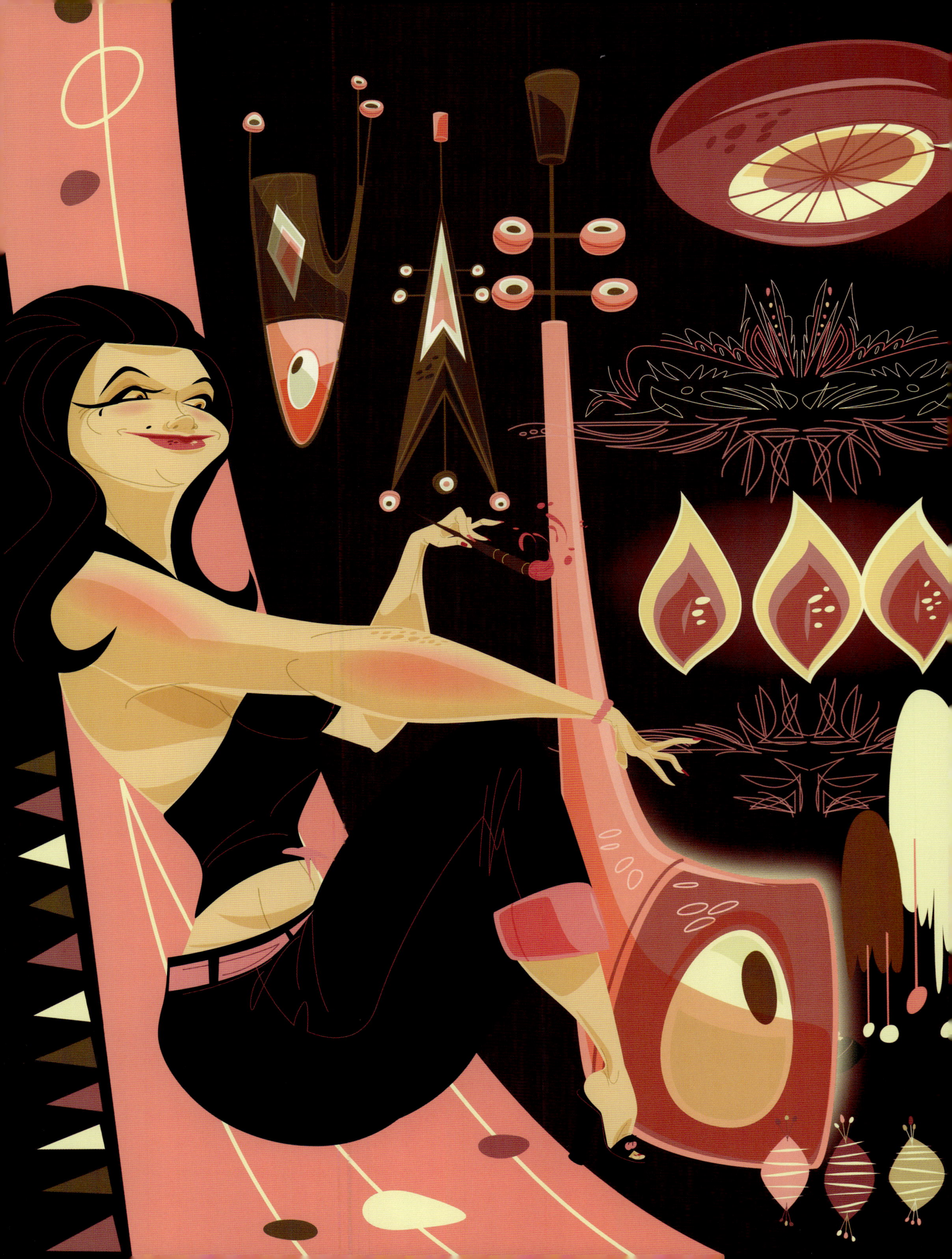

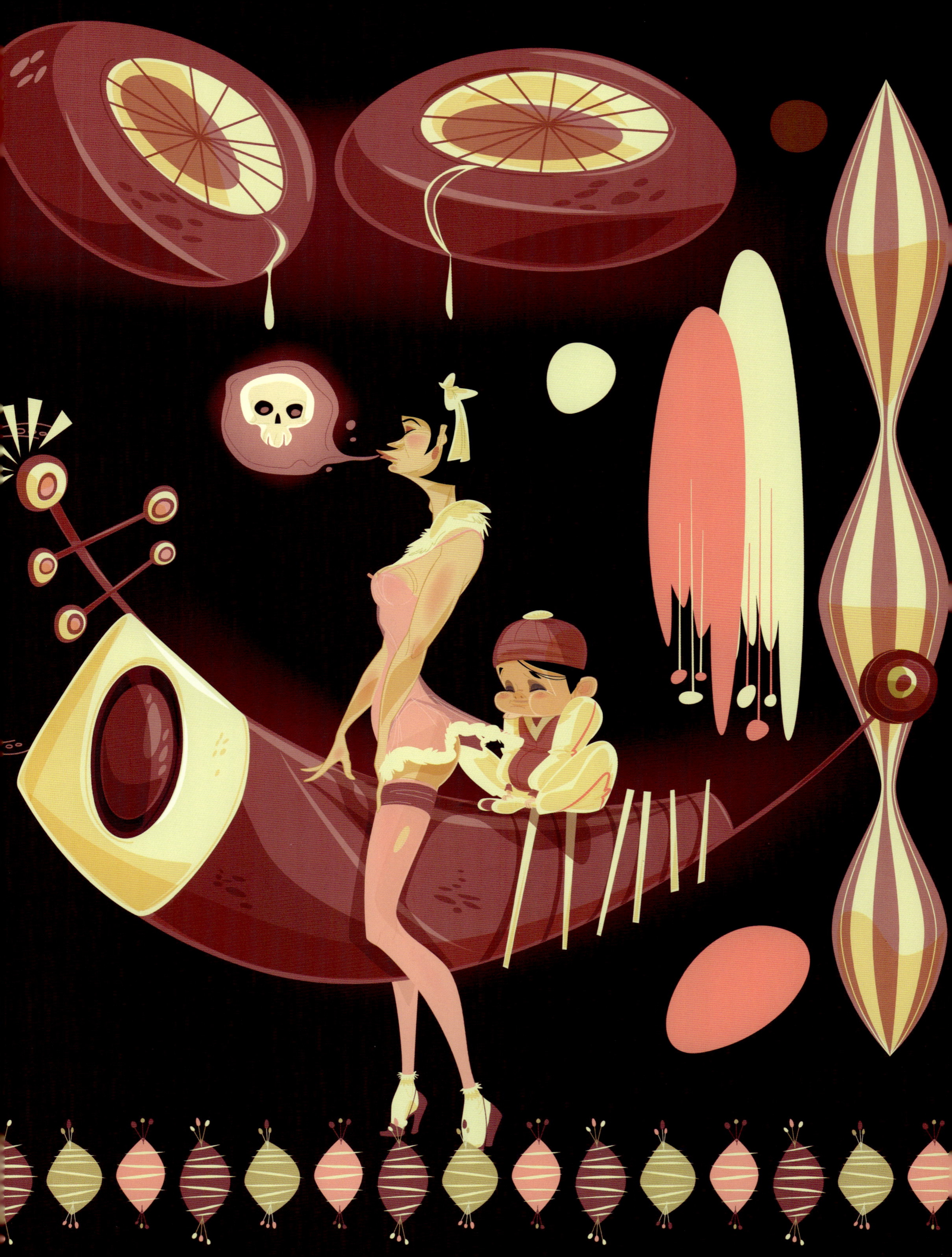

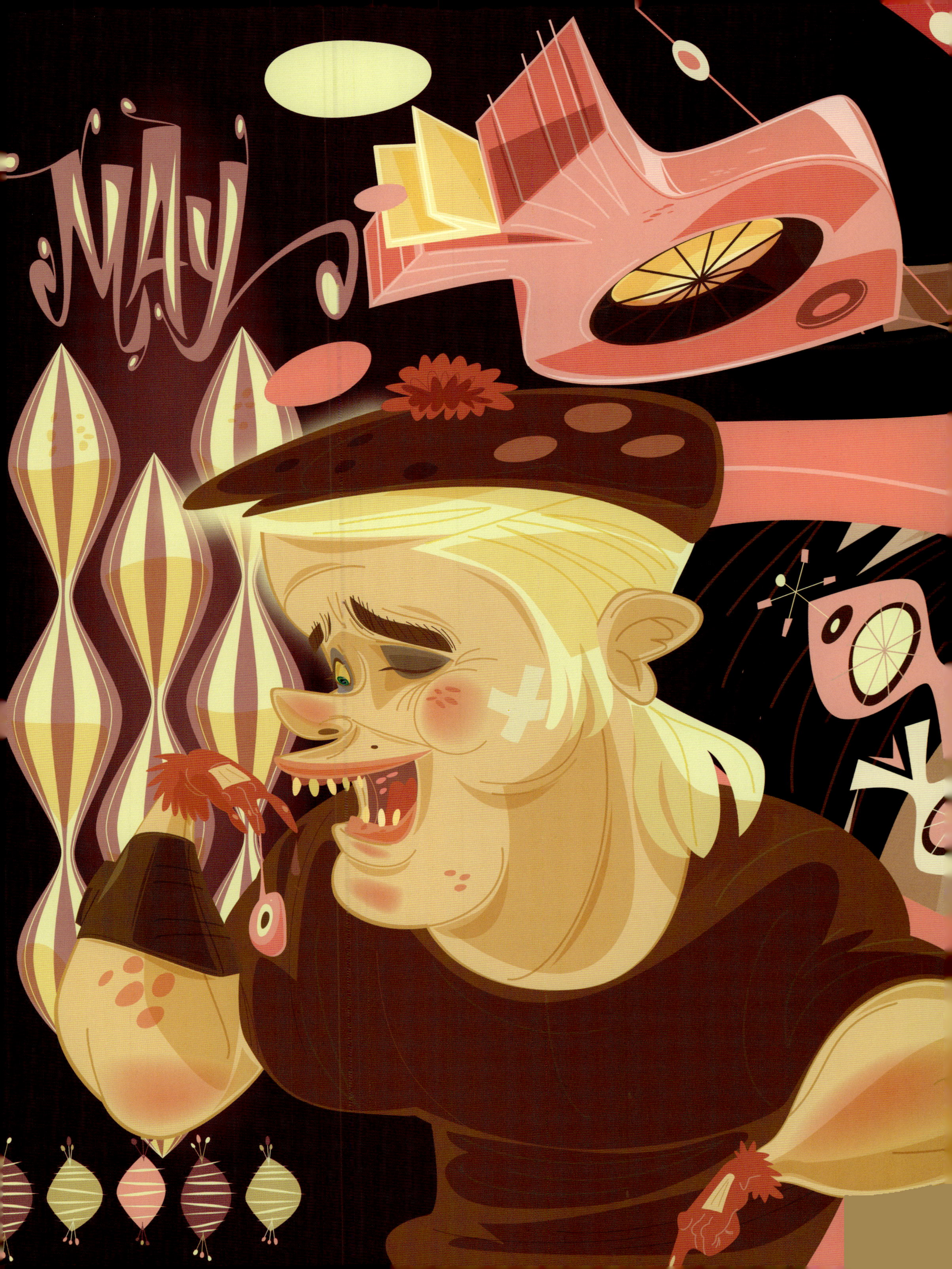
MAY

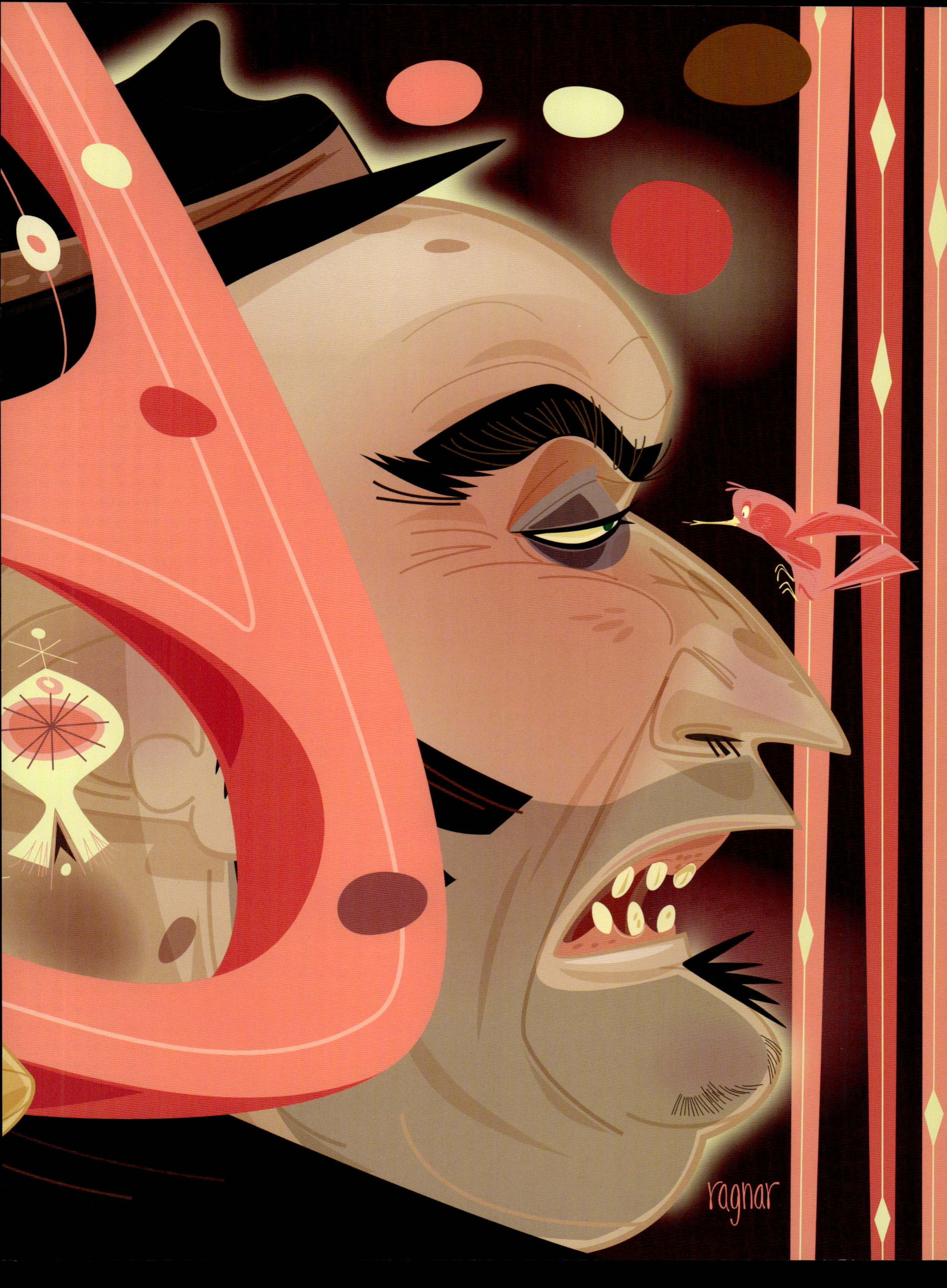
ragnar

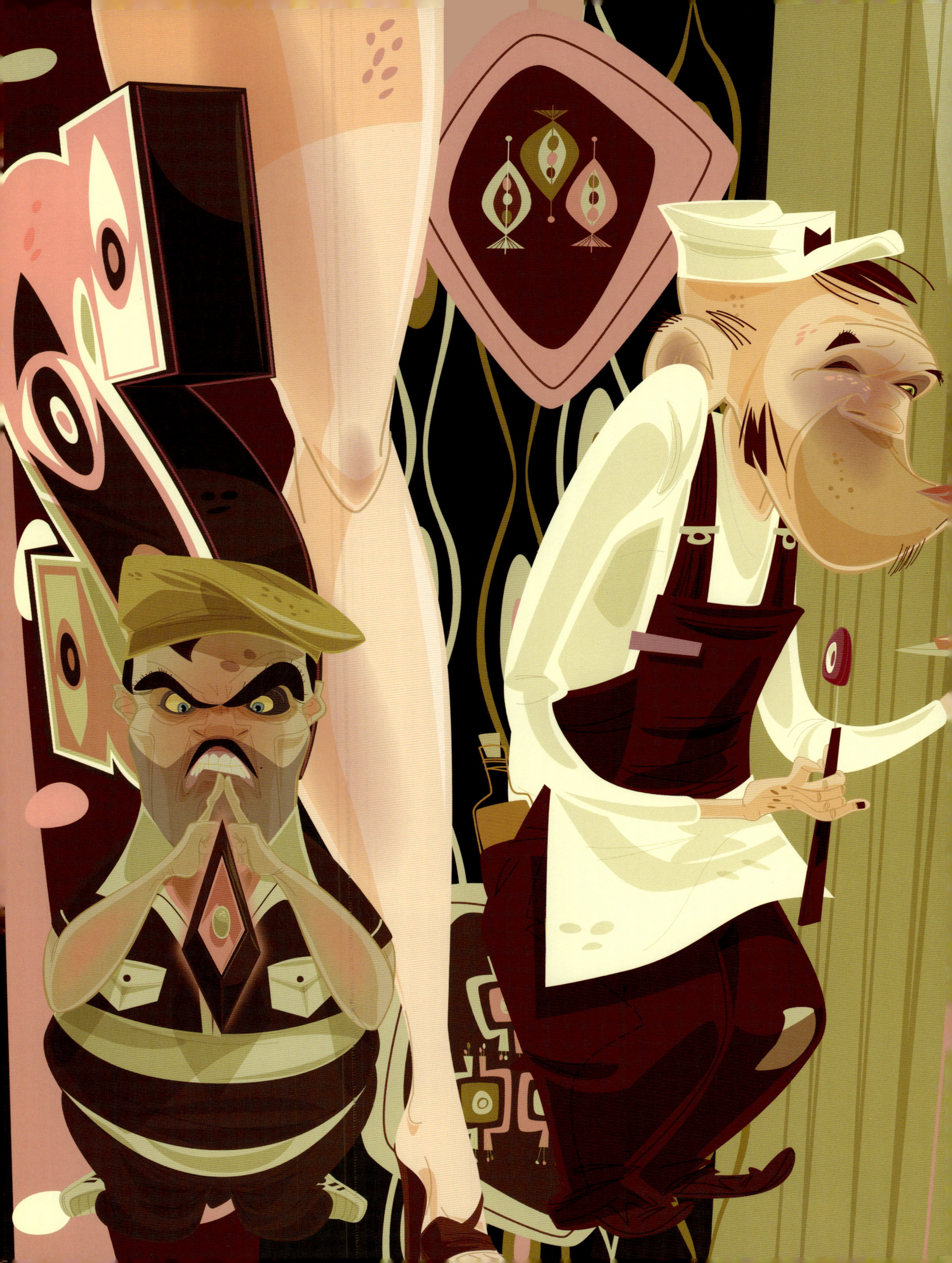

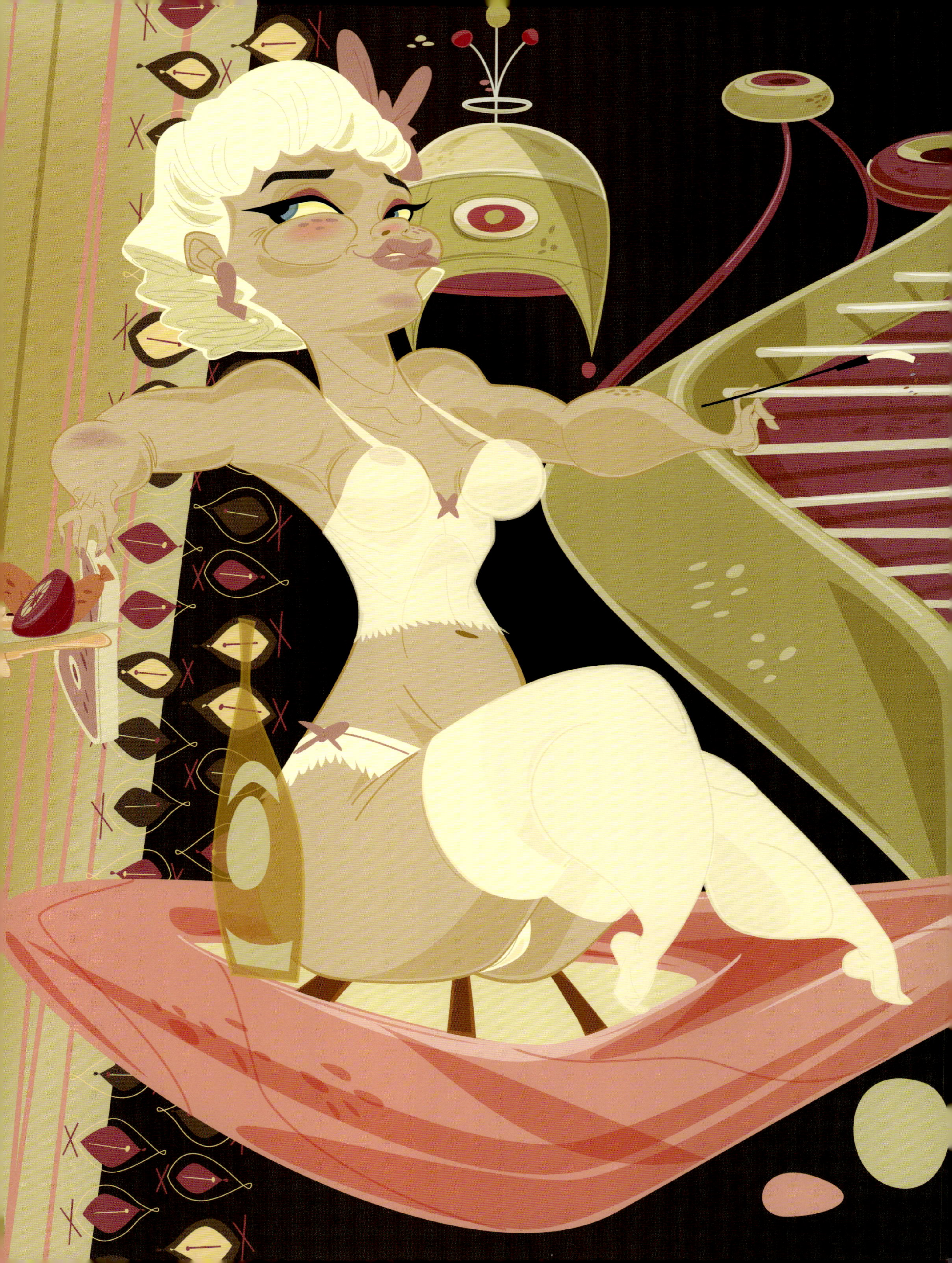

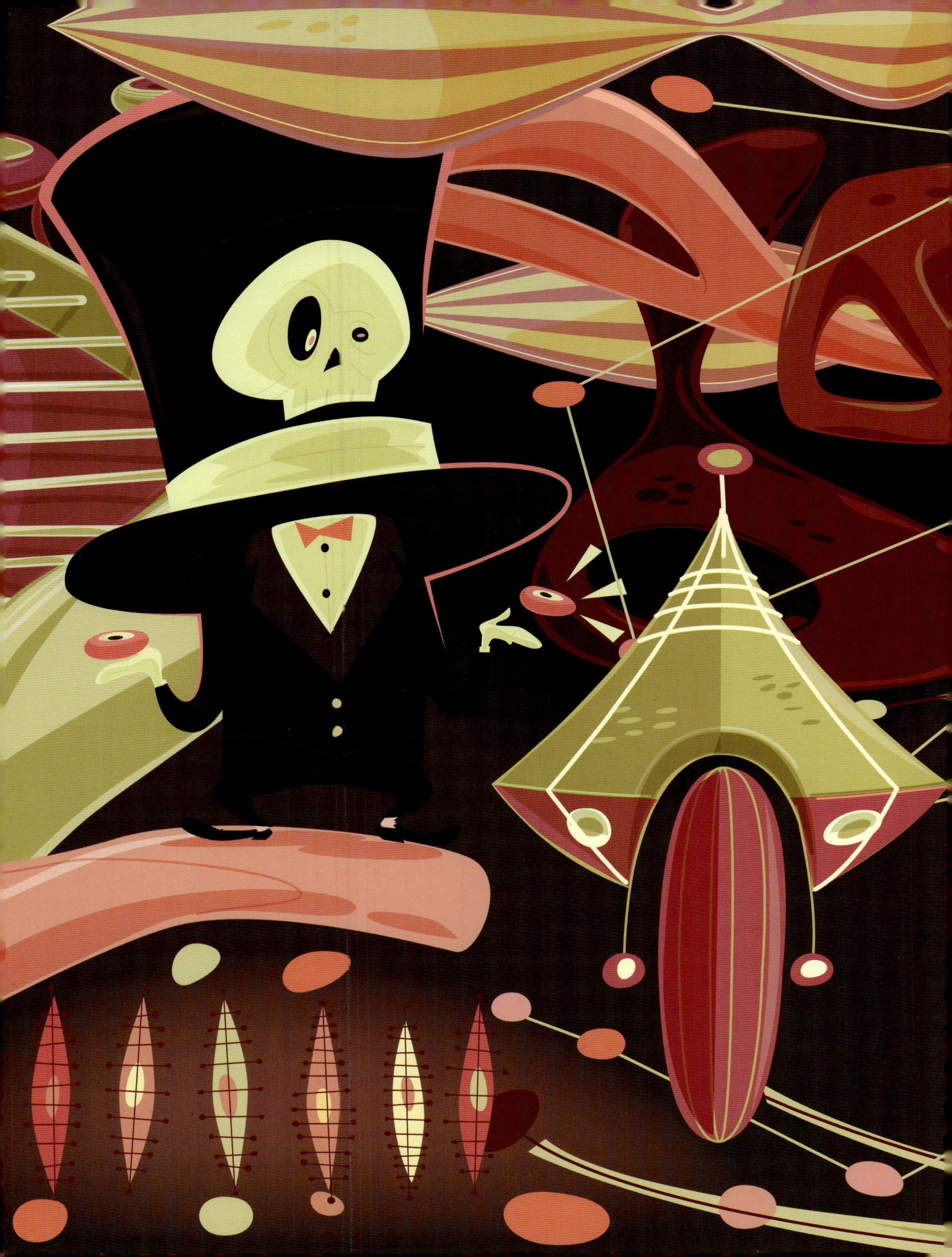

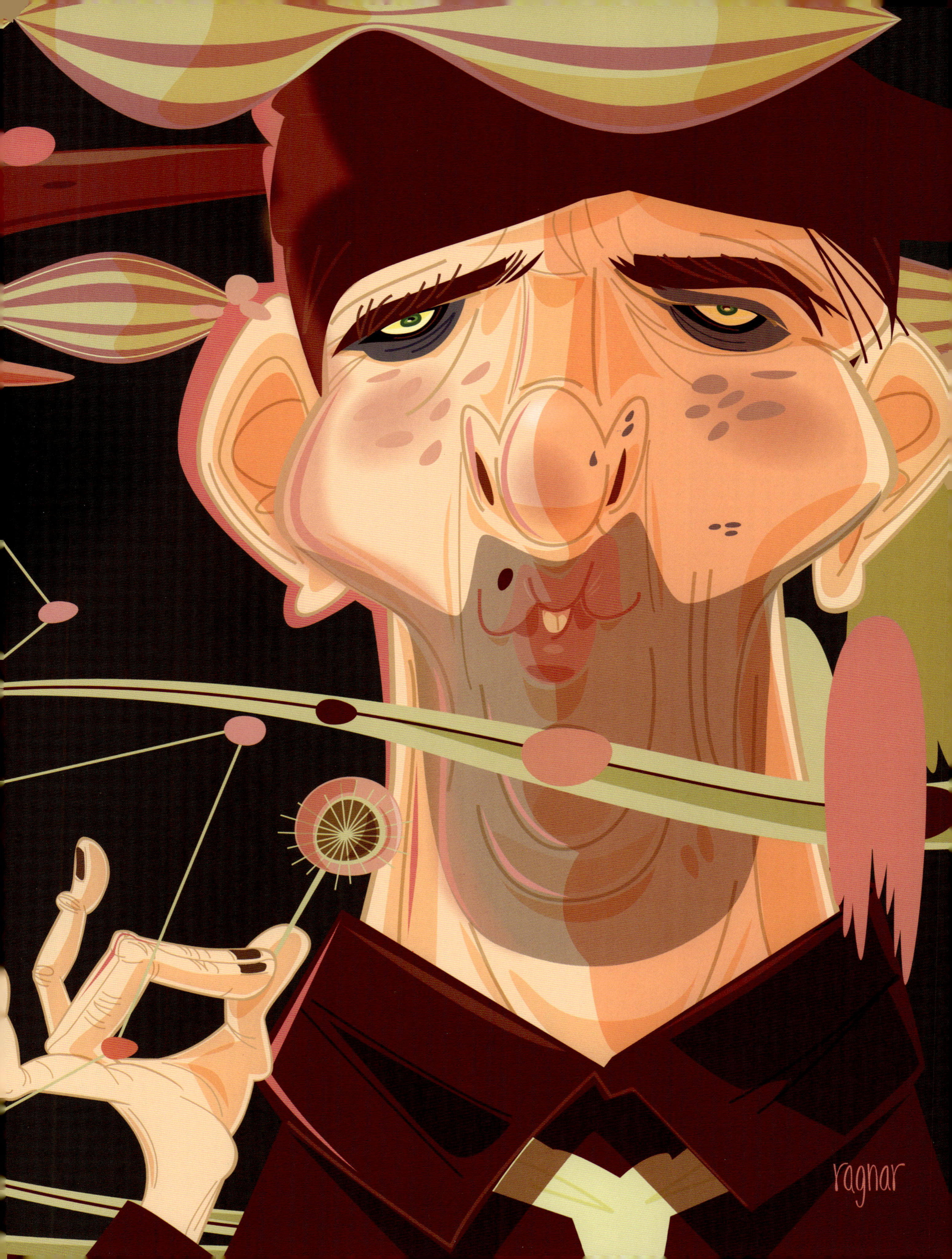
ragnar

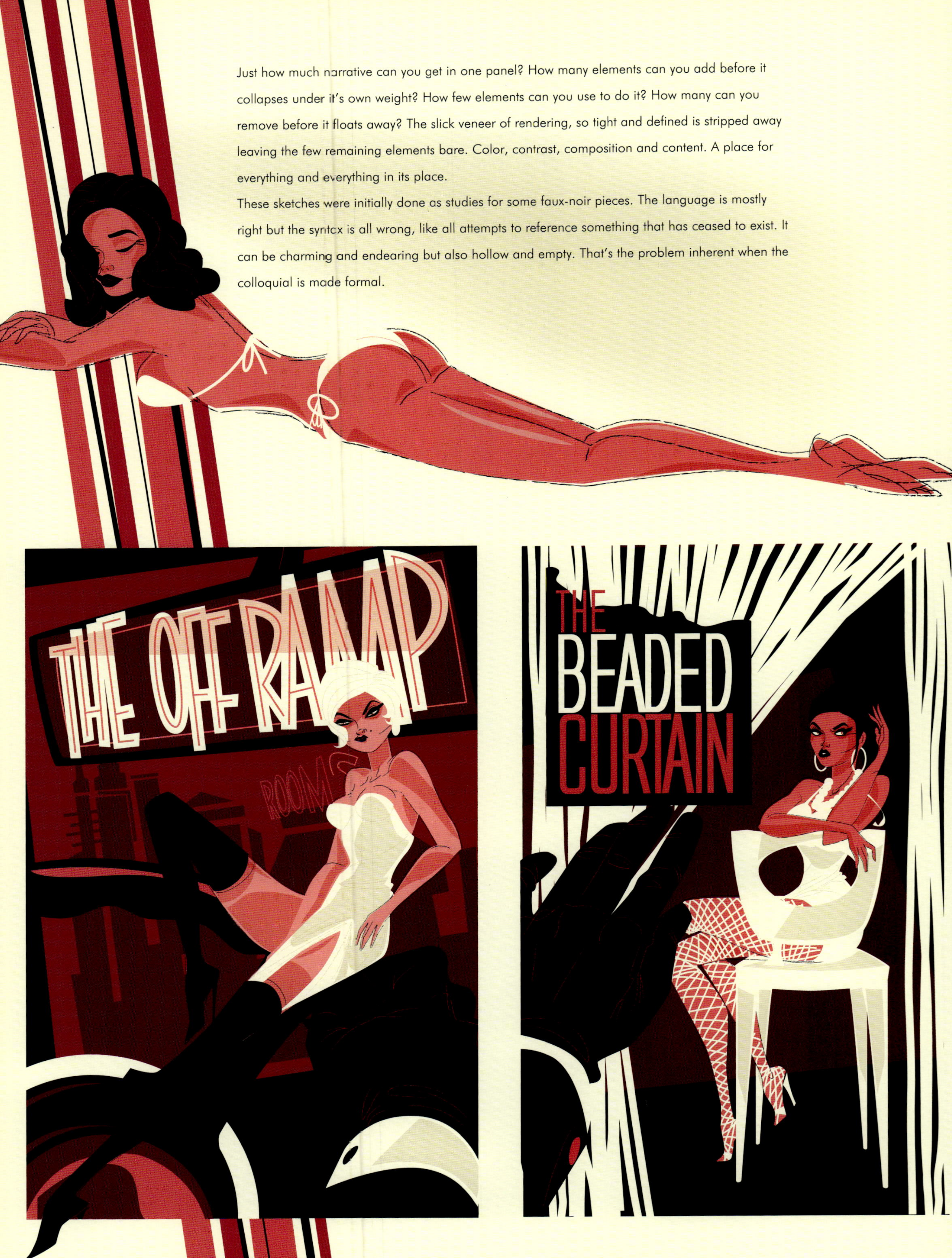

Just how much narrative can you get in one panel? How many elements can you add before it collapses under it's own weight? How few elements can you use to do it? How many can you remove before it floats away? The slick veneer of rendering, so tight and defined is stripped away leaving the few remaining elements bare. Color, contrast, composition and content. A place for everything and everything in its place.

These sketches were initially done as studies for some faux-noir pieces. The language is mostly right but the syntax is all wrong, like all attempts to reference something that has ceased to exist. It can be charming and endearing but also hollow and empty. That's the problem inherent when the colloquial is made formal.

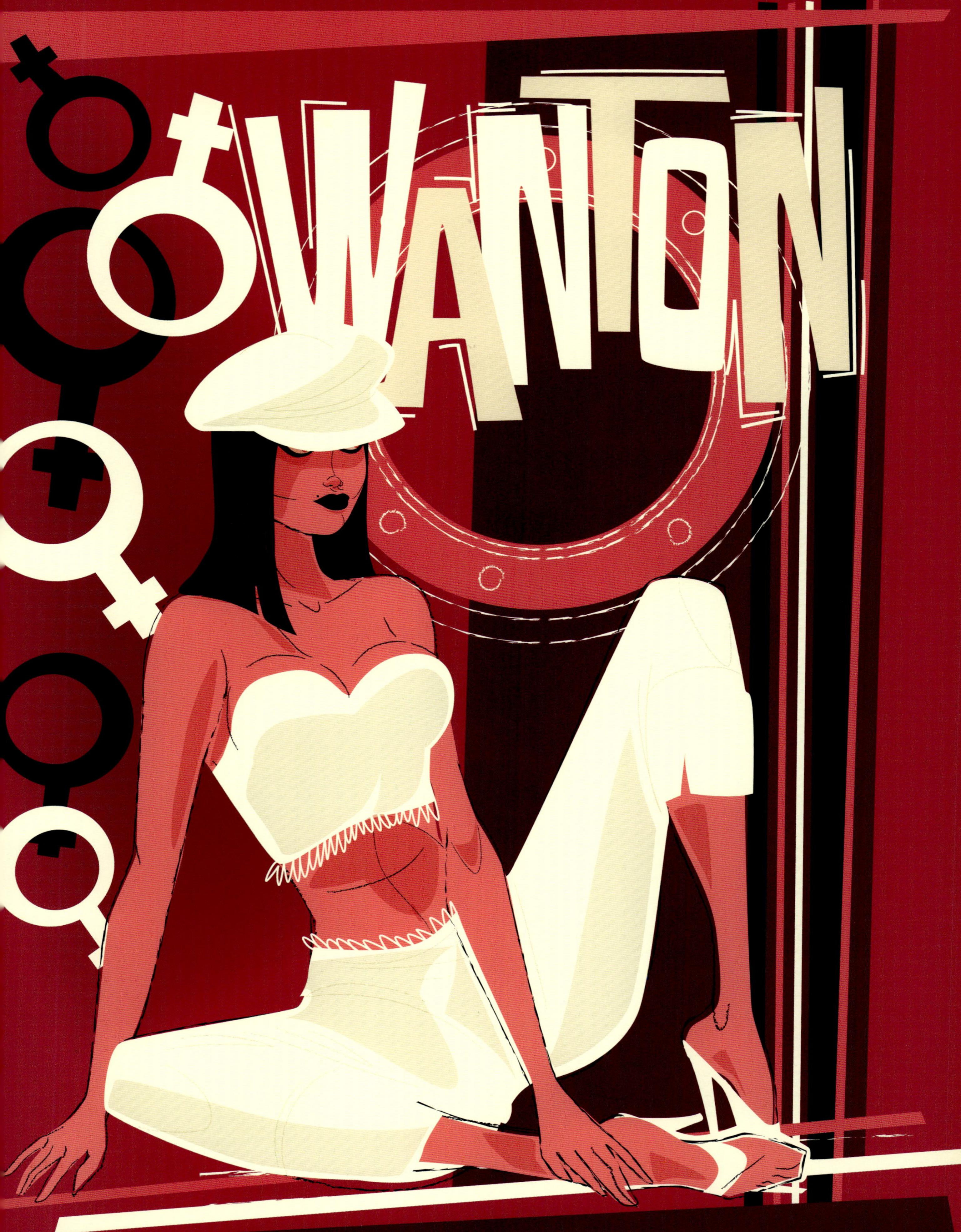

WANTON

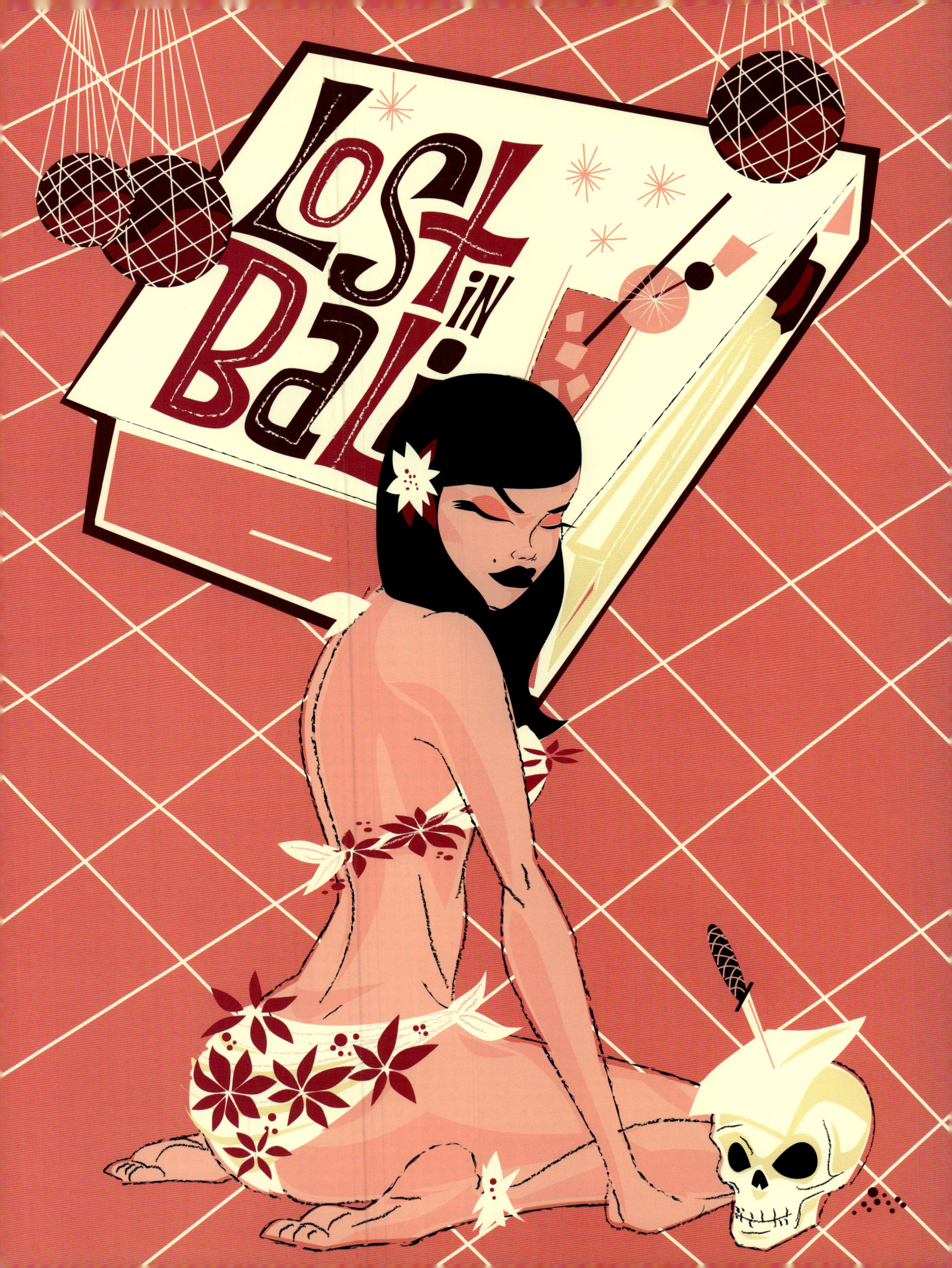

LOST in Bali

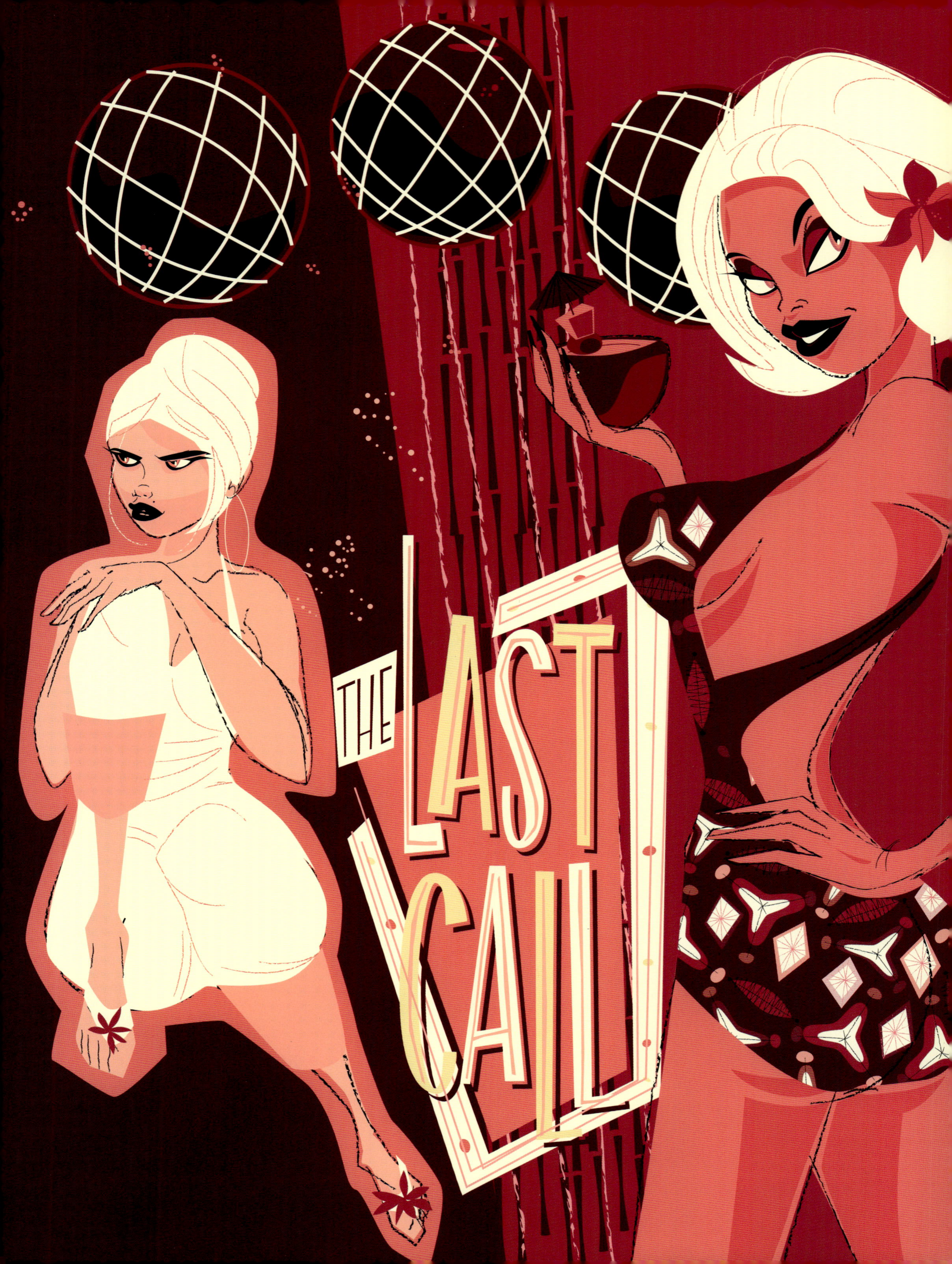

THE LAST CALL

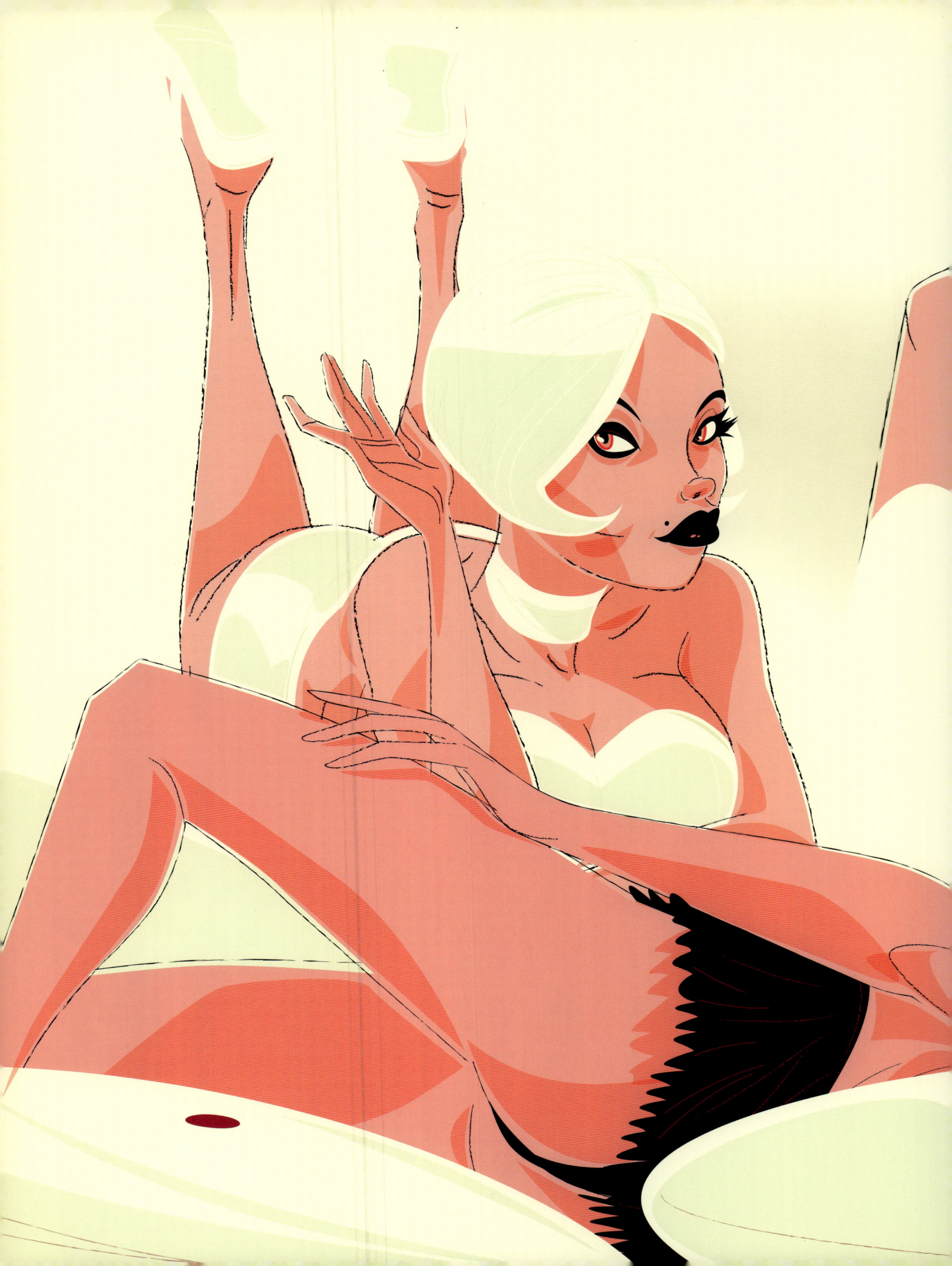

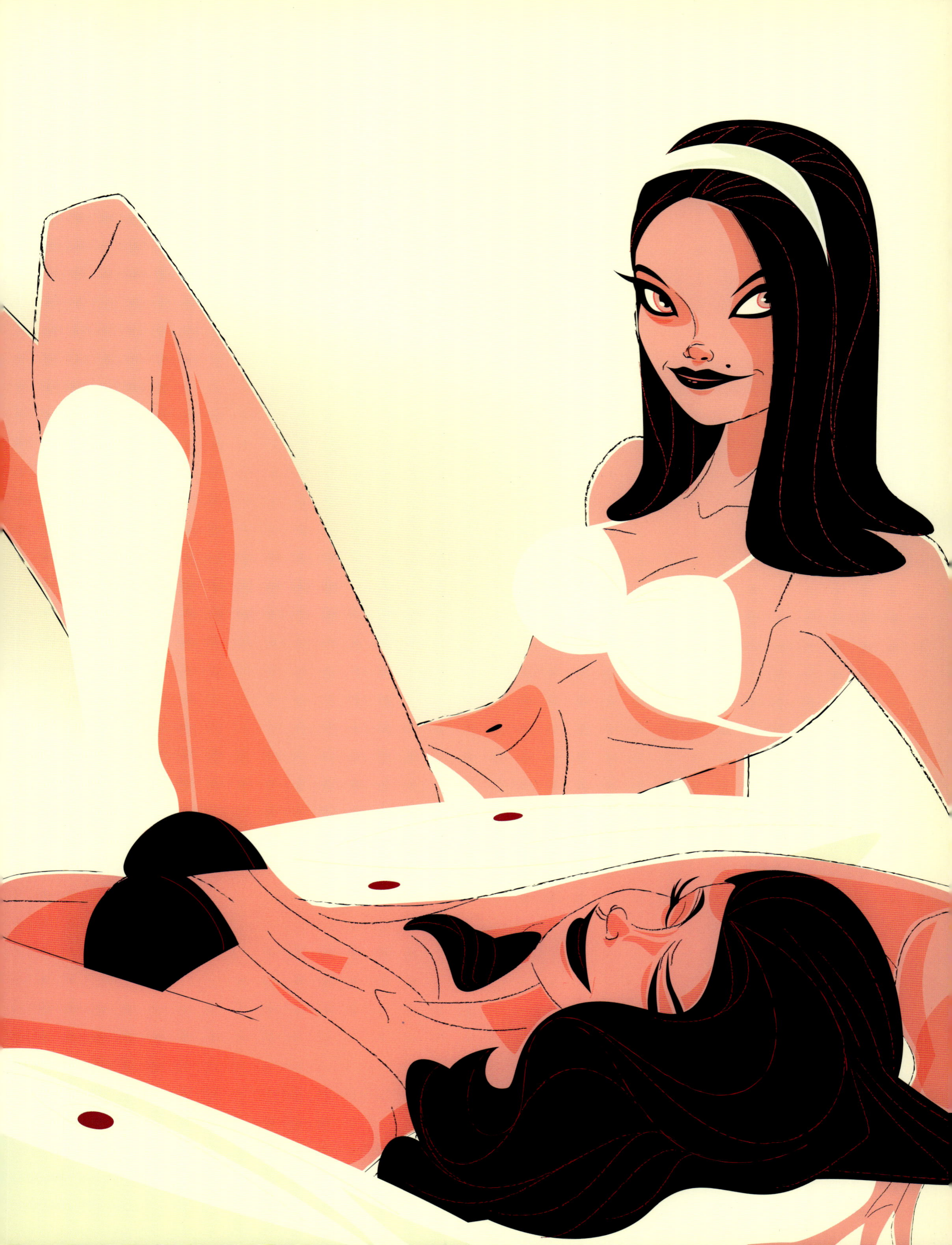

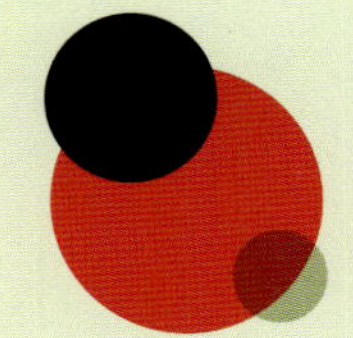

I owe a debt of gratitude and thanks to the following people-

My amazing wife and partner Jill and our kids- Oliver, Izzy and Montgomery.

Kathryn Johnson, Thure Johnson, Kym Pietch, Darren and Cathreen Johnson, Bob and Rani Self of Baby Tattoo,

Mike, Janeen, Phillip, Gabe, Nicole, Ken and Wanda at Van Eaton Galleries, Paul and Erik at House Of Secrets &

Art of Fiction, Joshua and Julie Leto, JJ Abrams, Thom Trainor, M Modern Gallery, Wind-Up Gallery, Dark Horse,

Jim Strader, Arnie and Cathy and Fenner, Tracy Lee and Electric Tiki, Robert Arce, Jim Gray and ACME Skateboards

and all the studios that kept me busy while not doing this stuff.